AnyTime Math™
Read-Aloud Anthology

□ HARCOURT BRACE & COMPANY □

Orlando Atlanta Austin Boston San Francisco Chicago Dallas New York
Toronto London

For permission to reprint copyrighted material, grateful acknowledgment is made to the following sources:

Alfred Publishing Co., Inc: Music and lyrics from "The Mexican Counting Song". Music and lyrics copyright © MCMLXIII by Highland Music Company. Copyright © assigned MCMXC to Alfred Publishing Co., Inc.
Dorothy Barker: "6 O'Clock Rooster" by Melvern Barker. Text copyright 1953 by Oxford University Press.
Boy Scouts of America: Music and lyrics from "One Finger, One Thumb" in *Boy Scout Songbook.* Music and lyrics copyright © 1970 by Boy Scouts of America.
Brimax Books, Newmarket, England: "One, Two, Three, Four, Five" from *Eric Kincaid's Book of Nursery Rhymes.* Text © 1985 by Brimax Rights Ltd.
Curtis Brown, Ltd.: Lyrics by Florence Parry Heide from "Wheels" in *Songs to Sing About Things You Think About.* Lyrics copyright © 1971 by Florence Parry Heide. Untitled poem (Retitled: "Monday/Muggy Day") from *Kim's Place and Other Poems* by Lee Bennett Hopkins. Text copyright © 1974 by Lee Bennett Hopkins.
Childrens Press: *Six Foolish Fishermen* by Benjamin Elkin. Text copyright © 1986 by Regensteiner Publishing Enterprises, Inc. Original text copyright © 1957 by Childrens Press,® Inc. Based on a folktale in Aston's Chap-Books of the Eighteenth Century, 1882.
T. S. Denison & Company, Inc: Music and lyrics from "Gum-Ball Machine" in *Action Songs and Rhythms for Children* by Lois Lunt Metz. Music and lyrics copyright © 1962 by T. S. Denison & Co., Inc.
Doubleday, a division of Bantam Doubleday Dell Publishing Group, Inc.: "The Animal Store" from *Taxis and Toadstools* by Rachel Field. Text copyright 1926 by Doubleday, a division of Bantam Doubleday Dell Publishing Group, Inc.
Dover Publications, Inc.: Illustrations by Sam Loyd from "The House That Jack Built" in *Tangrams—330 Puzzles* by Ronald C. Read. Copyright © 1965 by Dover Publications, Inc.
Dutton Children's Books, a division of Penguin Books USA Inc.: "The End" from *Now We Are Six* by A. A. Milne. Text copyright 1927 by E. P. Dutton, renewed © 1955 by A. A. Milne.
Farrar, Straus & Giroux, Inc.: "Two Friends" from *Spin a Soft Black Song* by Nikki Giovanni. Text copyright © 1971, 1985 by Nikki Giovanni.
Aileen Fisher: "The Furry Ones" by Aileen Fisher from *Feathered Ones and Furry.* Text copyright © 1971 by Aileen Fisher.
Frank Music Corp.: Music and lyrics from "The Inchworm" by Frank Loesser. Music and lyrics copyright © 1951, renewed © 1979 by Frank Music Corp.
Dee Gibson: Music and lyrics from "If You Had One Cat" by Dee Gibson in *Songs to Brighten Your Day* by Dee Gibson and Joe Scruggs.
Greenwillow Books, a division of William Morrow & Company, Inc.: *The Doorbell Rang* by Pat Hutchins. Copyright © 1986 by Pat Hutchins.
Gryphon House, Inc.: Untitled poems (Retitled: "Hippity-Hop" and "Every Morning") from *One Potato, Two Potato, Three Potato, Four,* compiled by Mary Lou Colgin. Text copyright © 1982 by Mary Louise N. Colgin.
Harcourt Brace & Company: *Koala Lou* by Mem Fox, illustrated by Pamela Lofts. Text copyright © 1988 by Mem Fox; illustrations copyright © 1988 by Pamela Lofts. Illustration by Walter Gaffney-Kessell from *The Sea Is Calling Me,* poems selected by Lee Bennett Hopkins. Illustration copyright © 1986 by Walter Gaffney-Kessell.
HarperCollins Publishers: Lyrics from "Springtime" in *Folk Songs of China, Japan, Korea,* edited by Betty Warner Dietz and Thomas Choonbai Park. Copyright © 1964 by The John Day Company, Inc. "Bedtime" from *Eleanor Farjeon's Poems for Children.* Text copyright 1933, renewed 1961 by Eleanor Farjeon. Originally published in *Over the Garden Wall* by Eleanor Farjeon. From *Arthur's Funny Money* by Lillian Hoban. Copyright © 1981 by Lillian Hoban. Untitled poems (Retitled: "High on a Hillside," "Ten Potatoes," "I'll Sing You a Song," and "A Tiny Wren in a Tree") from *Ten Potatoes in a Pot and Other Counting Rhymes* by Michael Jay Katz. Text copyright © 1990 by Michael Jay Katz. "Sitting in the Sand" and from "Tiptoe" in *Dogs & Dragons, Trees & Dreams* by Karla Kuskin. Text copyright © 1980 by Karla Kuskin. Untitled poem (Retitled: "Okay, Everybody") from *Near the Window Tree* by Karla Kuskin. Copyright © 1975 by Karla Kuskin. From "A Lost Button" in *Frog and Toad Are Friends* by Arnold Lobel. Copyright © 1970 by Arnold Lobel. Untitled poem (Retitled: "Pig With a Clock") from *The Book of Pigericks: Pig Limericks* by Arnold Lobel. Copyright © 1983 by Arnold Lobel. From "Very Tall Mouse and Very Short Mouse" in *Mouse Tales* by Arnold Lobel. Copyright © 1972 by Arnold Lobel. "Band-Aids" and "Smart" from *Where the Sidewalk Ends* by Shel Silverstein. Copyright © 1974 by Evil Eye Music, Inc. *Caps For Sale* by Esphyr Slobodkina. Copyright © 1940 and 1947, © renewed 1968 by Esphyr Slobodkina. Music and lyrics from "I'm Very, Very Tall" in *What Shall We Do and Allee Galloo!,* edited by Marie Winn, musical arrangements by Allan Miller. Music and lyrics copyright © 1970 by Marie Winn and Allan Miller.
Henry Holt and Company, Inc.: Untitled poems (Retitled: "One" and "Two") from *Everett Anderson's 1.2.3* by Lucille Clifton. Text copyright © 1977 by Lucille Clifton. *Two Ways to Count to Ten: A Liberian Folktale,* retold by Ruby Dee. Text copyright © 1988 by Ruby Dee.
Humanics Limited, Atlanta, GA: "Triangle" and "Rectangle" from *Fingerplays and Rhymes for Always and Sometimes* by Terry Lynne Graham. Text copyright © 1984 by Humanics Limited.
Klutz Press: Music and lyrics from "This Old Man" in *The Book of Kids Songs,* adapted by Nancy Cassidy. Music and lyrics copyright © 1986 by John and Nancy Cassidy.
Lothrop, Lee & Shepard Books, a division of William Morrow & Company, Inc.: Music from "The Mulberry Bush" and "Did You Ever See a Lassie?" in *Singing Bee!* by Jane Hart. Music copyright © 1982 by Jane Hart.
Gina Maccoby Literary Agency: "Money's Funny" from *Nuts to You and Nuts to Me* by Mary Ann Hoberman. Text copyright © 1974 by Mary Ann Hoberman. "How Many?," "How Far," "It's Dark Out," "Time," and "Birthdays" from *Yellow Butter Purple Jelly Red Jam Black Bread* by Mary Ann Hoberman. Text copyright © 1981 by Mary Ann Hoberman.
Macmillan Publishing Company: "Favorite Flower" from *It's About Time, Jesse Bear* by Nancy White Carlstrom. Text copyright © 1990 by Nancy White Carlstrom.
McFarland & Company, Inc., Publishers, Jefferson, NC 28640: "Three Balls," "One Potato, Two Potato," "Learning," "Two Little Blackbirds," and "Johnny's Hammers" from *Children's Counting-Out Rhymes, Fingerplays, Jump-Rope and Bounce-Ball Chants and Other Rhythms,* compiled by Gloria T. Delamar. Text copyright © 1983 by Gloria T. Delamar.
Rolf Myller: How Big Is a Foot? by Rolf Myller. Copyright © 1962, 1990 by Rolf Myller. Published by Dell Young Yearling, Dell Publishing.
Esther Nelson: Music from "Head and Shoulders, Knees and Toes" in *Musical Games for Children of All Ages* by Esther Nelson. Music © 1976 by Sterling Publishing Co., Inc.
Parker Publishing Company, Inc., a Division of Simon & Schuster, West Nyack, New York: Music and lyrics from "Rig-a-Jig-Jig" and "Navajo Happy Song" in *Musical Games, Fingerplays and Rhythmic Activities for Early Childhood* by Marian Wirth, Verna Stassevitch, Rita Shotwell and Patricia Stemmler. Music and lyrics © 1983 by Parker Publishing Company, Inc.
Philomel Books: "Sharing" from *Catch Me & Kiss Me & Say It Again* by Clyde Watson. Text copyright © 1978 by Clyde Watson.
Marian Reiner, on behalf of Myra Cohn Livingston: "Feet" and "Tails" from *A Song I Sang to You* by Myra Cohn Livingston. Text copyright © 1984, 1969, 1967, 1965, 1959, 1958 by Myra Cohn Livingston.
Marian Reiner, on behalf of Lilian Moore: "Telling Time" from *Think of Shadows* by Lilian Moore. Text copyright © 1975, 1980 by Lilian Moore.
Marian Reiner: Untitled poem (Retitled: "How Do You Make a Pizza Grow?") from *Blackberry Ink* by Eve Merriam. Text copyright © 1985 by Eve Merriam. "Hurry" from *Out Loud* by Eve Merriam. Text copyright © 1973 by Eve Merriam. "A Poem for a Pickle" from *A Poem for a Pickle* by Eve Merriam. Text copyright © 1989 by Eve Merriam.
Elizabeth M. Roach: "Dogs" and "Our Tree" from *Around and About* by Marchette Chute. Text copyright 1957 by E. P. Dutton; text copyright renewed 1984 by Marchette Chute.
Scholastic Inc.: "The Graceful Elephant"/"Un elefante se balanceaba" from *Arroz Con Leche: Popular Songs and Rhymes from Latin America,* selected by Lulu Delacre. Text copyright © 1989 by Lulu Delacre. "How Many Spots Does a Leopard Have?" from *How Many Spots Does a Leopard Have? and Other Tales* by Julius Lester. Text copyright © 1989 by Julius Lester.
Michael Seeger, on behalf of Ruth Crawford Seeger: Music and lyrics from "Clap Your Hands" in *American Folk Songs for Children* by Ruth Crawford Seeger. Music and lyrics copyright 1948 by Ruth Crawford Seeger. Published by Doubleday & Company, Inc.
Sidgwick and Jackson, Ltd.: "Choosing Shoes" from *The Very Thing* by Ffrida Wolfe. Published by Sidgwick and Jackson, Ltd., 1928.
Simon & Schuster, New York: Music and lyrics from "The Hokey Pokey" in *The Fireside Book of Children's Songs,* collected and edited by Marie Winn, musical arrangements by Allan Miller. Music and lyrics copyright © 1966 by Marie Winn and Allan Miller.
Songs Music, Inc., Scarborough, NY 10510: Music and lyrics from "Five Little Ducks" in *Eye Winker Tom Tinker Chin Chopper: Fifty Musical Fingerplays* by Tom Glazer. Music and lyrics © by Songs Music, Inc. Published by Doubleday.
William Van Clief: Music by Sylvia Worth Van Clief from "Wheels" in *Songs to Sing About Things You Think About.* Music © 1971 by Sylvia Worth Van Clief.
Warren-Mattox Productions: Music and lyrics from "Mary Mack" and "Bluebird, Bluebird" in *Shake It to the One That You Love the Best,* adapted by Cheryl Warren Mattox. Music and lyrics copyright © 1989 by Warren-Mattox Productions.
Western Publishing Company, Inc.: "I Like Cars" and "I Like Dogs" from *The Friendly Book* by Margaret Wise Brown. Text © 1954 by Western Publishing Company, Inc.
The H. W. Wilson Company, New York: "Counting Crocodiles" and "Peace and Quiet" from *The Flannel Board Storytelling Book* by Judy Sierra. Text copyright © 1987 by Judy Sierra.

Printed in the United States of America

ISBN 0-15-305398-4

1 2 3 4 5 6 7 8 9 10 048 97 96 95 94

Table of Contents

POEMS and RHYMES

POEMS AND RHYMES

Five pennies for a nickel,
a poem for a pickle...

From "A Poem for a Pickle"
by *Eve Merriam*
page 32

Two Friends

lydia and shirley have

two pierced ears and two bare ones

five pigtails

two pairs of sneakers two berets

two smiles

one necklace

one bracelet

lots of stripes and

one good friendship

Nikki Giovanni

I Like Dogs

Big dogs　　　Little dogs
　Fat dogs　　　Doggy dogs
　　Old dogs　　　Puppy dogs

I like dogs
A dog that is barking over the hill
A dog that is dreaming very still
A dog that is running wherever he will
I like dogs.

Margaret Wise Brown

Five Little Chickens

Said the first little chicken,
    With a queer little squirm,
"I wish I could find
    A fat little worm."

Said the next little chicken,
    With an odd little shrug,
"I wish I could find
    A fat little bug."

Said the third little chicken,
    With a sharp little squeal,
"I wish I could find
    Some nice yellow meal."

Said the fourth little chicken,
    With a small sigh of grief,
"I wish I could find
    A little green leaf."

Said the fifth little chicken,
    With a faint little moan,
"I wish I could find
    A wee gravel stone."

Said the old mother hen
    From the green garden patch
"If you want any breakfast,
    Just come here and scratch."

I Like Cars

I like cars
Red cars   Green cars
Sport limousine cars

I like cars
A car in a garage
A car with a load
A car with a flat tire
A car on the road
I like cars.

Margaret Wise Brown

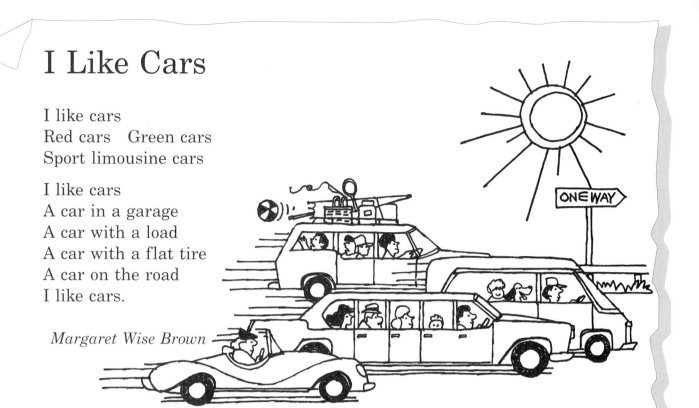

Dogs

The dogs I know
Have many shapes.
For some are big and tall,
    And some are long,
    And
    some
    are thin,
And some are fat and small.

And some are little bits of fluff
And have no shape at all.

Marchette Chute

Tails

A dog's tail
  is short
And a cat's tail
  is long,
And a horse has a tail
  that he
  swishes along,
And a fish has a tail
  that can
  help him
  to swim,
And a pig has a tail
  that looks
  curly on him.

All monkeys have tails
And all lions and whales
There is
simply no
end
to
    the
        number
            of
                tails!

Myra Cohn Livingston

5

The Furry Ones

I like —
the furry ones —
the waggy ones
the purry ones
the hoppy ones
that hurry,

The glossy ones
the saucy ones
the sleepy ones
the leapy ones
the mousy ones
that scurry,

The snuggly ones
the huggly ones
the never, never
ugly ones . . .
all soft
and warm
and furry.

Aileen Fisher

6

Favorite Flower

Flowers in a bed
Flowers in a row
Flowers on the fence
Watch them grow.

Some stand tiny
Some stand tall
Some hang over
And others crawl.

Bee flowers
Tree flowers
Flowers on a vine

Flowers in the morning
Flowers all the time.

Yellow flowers
Orange flowers
Purple, red and blue.

I pick my favorite flower
And give it to you.

Nancy White Carlstrom

Choosing Shoes

New shoes, new shoes,
    Red and pink and blue shoes.
Tell me, what would *you* choose,
    If they'd let us buy?

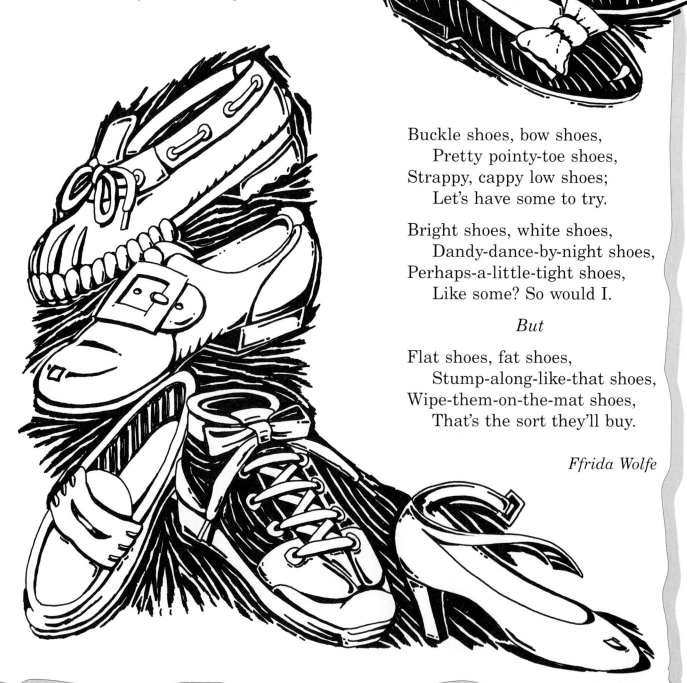

Buckle shoes, bow shoes,
    Pretty pointy-toe shoes,
Strappy, cappy low shoes;
    Let's have some to try.

Bright shoes, white shoes,
    Dandy-dance-by-night shoes,
Perhaps-a-little-tight shoes,
    Like some? So would I.

But

Flat shoes, fat shoes,
    Stump-along-like-that shoes,
Wipe-them-on-the-mat shoes,
    That's the sort they'll buy.

Ffrida Wolfe

8

Every Morning

Every morning at eight o'clock
You can hear the mailman's knock.
Up jumps Katy to open the door,
One letter, two letters, three letters,
FOUR.

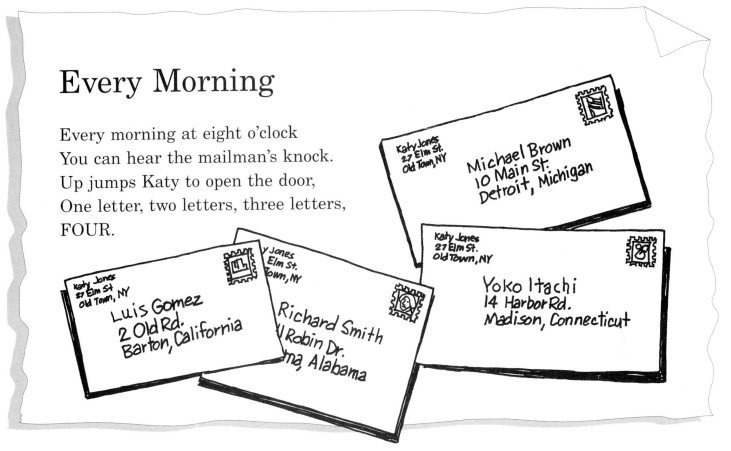

One,
Two,
Three,
Four,
Five

One, two, three, four, five,
Once I caught a fish alive,
Six, seven, eight, nine, ten,
Then I let it go again.

Why did you let it go?
Because it bit my finger so.
Which finger did it bite?
This little finger on the right.

One Potato,
Two Potato

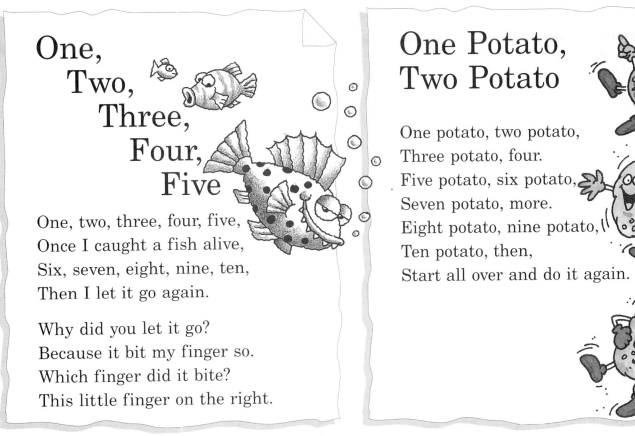

One potato, two potato,
Three potato, four.
Five potato, six potato,
Seven potato, more.
Eight potato, nine potato,
Ten potato, then,
Start all over and do it again.

Johnny's Hammers

Johnny works with *one* hammer,
One hammer, one hammer,
Johnny works with one hammer,
Then he works with *two.*

Johnny works with *two* hammers,
Two hammers, two hammers,
Johnny works with two hammers,
Then he works with *three.*

Johnny works with *three* hammers,
Three hammers, three hammers,
Johnny works with three hammers,
Then he works with *four.*

Johnny works with *four* hammers,
Four hammers, four hammers,
Johnny works with *four* hammers,
Then he works with *five.*

Johnny works with *five* hammers,
Five hammers, five hammers,
Johnny works with five hammers,
Then he goes to *sleep.*

One

One can eat a whole candy bar alone.
One can win a race.
One can have a drum of his own
or can go someplace
without Mama! One can have fun
alone, says Everett Anderson.

Lucille Clifton

Two

Everett Anderson says, Thank you,
but I have gotten used to Two.
Two at dinner,
Two flying kites,
Two at market,
Two at night, and
I'm not lonely at all, thank you,
I have gotten used to Two.

Lucille Clifton

The End

When I was One,
I had just begun.

When I was Two,
I was nearly new.

When I was Three,
I was hardly Me.

When I was Four,
I was not much more.

When I was Five,
I was just alive.

But now I am Six, I'm as clever as clever.
So I think I'll be six now for ever and ever.

A. A. Milne

How Many?

A mother skunk all black and white
Leads her babies down the street
    Pitter patter
    Pitter patter
    Pitter patter
    TWENTY feet.

Off they toddle slow and steady
Making tiny twitter cries
    Flitter flutter
    Flitter flutter
    Flitter flutter
    TEN small eyes.

Nose to tail-tip in procession
Single-file the family trails
    Flippy floppy
    Flippy floppy
    Flippy floppy
    FIVE long tails.

Up the street a dog comes barking,
Sees the strangers, leaps pell-mell . . .
    Ickle pickle
    Ickle pickle
    Ickle pickle
    ONE BIG SMELL!

Mary Ann Hoberman

High on a Hillside

High on a hillside
Brown as bread,
Emmy found a berry patch
Spotted all in red.

Raspberries, raspberries,
Thick as fireflies,
Dotting all the bushes
Like stars in the skies.

"One, two, twenty, sixty deep—
A fifteen hundred berry heap."
Emmy tried to count them all
But soon she fell asleep.

Two Little Blackbirds

Two little blackbirds
Sitting on a hill.
One was named Jack
And one was named Jill.
Fly away Jack,
Fly away Jill,
Come back Jack,
Come back Jill.
Two little blackbirds
Sitting on a hill.

The Graceful Elephant

A Mexican folk rhyme

One elephant balanced gracefully
Upon a spider's web,
But when the web bounced him all around
He called in another to help hold it down.

Two elephants balanced gracefully
Upon a spider's web,
But when the web bounced them all around
They called in another to help hold it down.

Three elephants . . .
Four elephants . . .
Etc. . . .

Un elefante se balanceaba

Un elefante se balanceaba
sobre la tela de una araña,
como veía que resistía
fue a llamar a otro elefante.

Dos elefantes se balanceaban
sobre la tela de una araña,
como veían que resistía
fueron a llamar a otro elefante.

Tres elefantes . . .
Cuatro elefantes . . .
Etc. . . .

A Tiny Wren in a Tree

A tiny wren sat in a tree.
Whistle, and she'll come to thee.
Two more hopped in—then there were three.
Whistle, child, before they flee.

Another came, and there were four
But you needn't whistle anymore;
For, being frightened, off they flew,
And none are left to play with you.

I'll Sing You a Song

If you listen, I'll sing you a song,
And I would guess that it's nine verses long—
I'll give you a pin if I've guessed wrong.

Three and three and three are nine—
And if I don't forget a line,
I guess the pin will still be mine.

Band-Aids

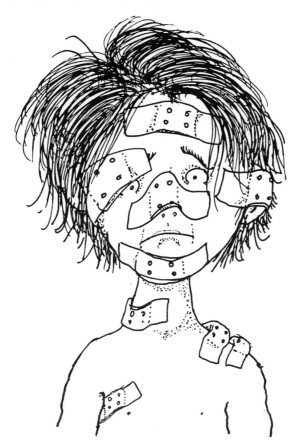

I have a Band-Aid on my finger,
One on my knee, and one on my nose,
One on my heel, and two on my shoulder,
Three on my elbow, and nine on my toes.
Two on my wrist, and one on my ankle,
One on my chin, and one on my thigh,
Four on my belly, and five on my bottom,
One on my forehead, and one on my eye.
One on my neck, and in case I might need 'em
I have a box full of thirty-five more.
But oh! I do think it's sort of a pity
I don't have a cut or a sore!

Shel Silverstein

Ten Potatoes

Ten potatoes in a pot,
Take two out and eight stay hot.
Eight potatoes in the pan,
Take two out, there's six to plan.
Six potatoes on the stove,
Take two off and four's the trove.
Four potatoes in the kettle,
Take two out, leave two to settle.
Two potatoes still aboil,
Take them out before they spoil.

How Do You Make a
Pizza Grow?

How do you make a pizza grow?

You pound and you pull and you stretch the dough
And throw in tomatoes and oregano.

Pizza platter for twenty-two,
Pour on the oil and soak it through.

Pizza slices for forty-four,
Chop up onions, make some more.

Pizza pie for sixty-six
With mozzarella cheese that melts and sticks.

Pizza pizza for ninety-nine
With pepperoni sausage ground-up fine.

Pizza pizza stretch the dough,
Pizza pizza make it grow.

Eve Merriam

Okay Everybody

Okay everybody, listen to this:

I am tired of being smaller

Than you

And them

And him

And trees and buildings.

So watch out

All you gorillas and adults

Beginning tomorrow morning

Boy

Am I going to be taller.

Karla Kuskin

Sitting in the Sand

Sitting in the sand and the sea comes up

So you put your hands together

And you use them like a cup

And you dip them in the water

With a scooping kind of motion

And before the sea goes out again

You have a sip of ocean.

Karla Kuskin

Telling Time

Time ticks,
whispers,
rings,
sounds a chime,
a ping,
a tock,
or the long slow
bong
of a grandfather clock.

Time
on the sundial
is a
shadow,
making its rounds,
moving
till day is done
in secret
understanding
with the sun.

Lilian Moore

Time

Listen to the clock strike
One
     two
          three,
Up in the tall tower
One
     two
          three.
Hear the hours slowly chime;
Watch the hands descend and climb;
Listen to the sound of time
One
     two
          three.

Mary Ann Hoberman

It's Dark Out

It's dark out
It's dark out
Although the hour's early;
It isn't even five o'clock
And yet it's dark all down the block
Because the season's winter
And the sun has gone to bed.

Mary Ann Hoberman

Tiptoe

Yesterday I skipped all day,
The day before I ran,
Today I'm going to tiptoe
Everywhere I can.

Karla Kuskin

Hurry

Hurry! says the morning,
Don't be late for school!

Hurry! says the teacher,
Hand in papers now!

Hurry! says the mother,
Supper's getting cold!

Hurry! says the father,
Time to go to bed!

slowly, says the darkness,
you can talk to me . . .

Eve Merriam

Birthdays

If birthdays happened once a week

Instead of once a year,

Think of all the gifts you'd get

And all the songs you'd hear

And think how quickly you'd grow up;

Wouldn't it feel queer

If birthdays happened once a week

Instead of once a year?

Mary Ann Hoberman

Feet

Feet are very special things
For special kinds of fun.

On weekdays they walk off to school
Or skip—or hop—or run—

On Saturdays they roller-skate
Or bicycle—or hike—

On Sundays they just do the things
That other people like.

Myra Cohn Livingston

How Far

How far
How far
How far is today
When tomorrow has come
and it's yesterday?

Far
And far
And far away.

Mary Ann Hoberman

Bedtime

Five minutes, five minutes more, please!
    Let me stay five minutes more!
Can't I just finish the castle
    I'm building here on the floor?
Can't I just finish the story
    I'm reading here in my book?
Can't I just finish this bead-chain—
    It *almost* is finished, look!
Can't I just finish this game, please?
    When a game's once begun
It's a pity never to find out
    Whether you've lost or won.
Can't I just stay five minutes?
    Well, can't I stay just four?
Three minutes, then? two minutes?
    Can't I stay *one* minute more?

Eleanor Farjeon

Pig with a Clock

There was an old pig with a clock

Who experienced anguish and shock,

For he greased it with butter,

Which caused it to sputter

And drowned both its tick and its tock.

Arnold Lobel

Our Tree

When spring comes round, our apple tree
    Is very full of flowers,
And when a bird sits on a branch
    The petals fall in showers.

When summer comes, our apple tree
    Is very full of green,
And everywhere you look in it
    There is a leafy screen.

When autumn comes, our apple tree
    Is full of things to eat.
The apples hang from every branch
    To tumble at our feet.

When winter comes, our apple tree
    Is full of snow and ice
And rabbits come to visit it . . .
    We think our tree is nice.

Marchette Chute

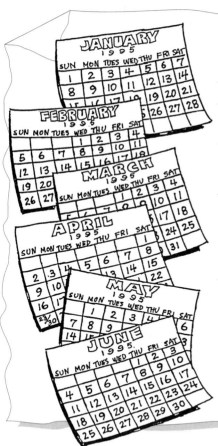

Months of the Year

Thirty days has
   September,
April, June, and
   November;
February has
   twenty-eight alone,
All the rest have
   thirty-one,
Excepting leap year,
   that's the time
When February's days
   are twenty-nine.

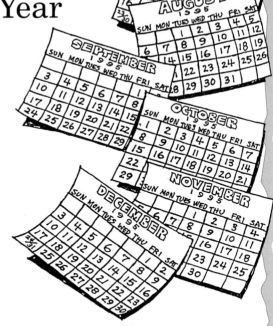

Monday/Muggy-day

Monday/Muggy-day
Tuesday/Tornado-day
Wednesday/Windy-day
Thursday/Thunder-day
Friday/Foggy-day
Saturday/Soggy-day
Sunday

   At last!

SUN

   day

Lee Bennett Hopkins

Los días de la semana

Lunes, martes, miércoles, ¡tres!
Jueves, viernes, sábado, ¡seis!
Domingo, siete, ¡que fiesta es!

The Days of the Week

Monday, Tuesday, Wednesday, three!
Thursday, Friday, Saturday, six!
Sunday, seven; what a party!

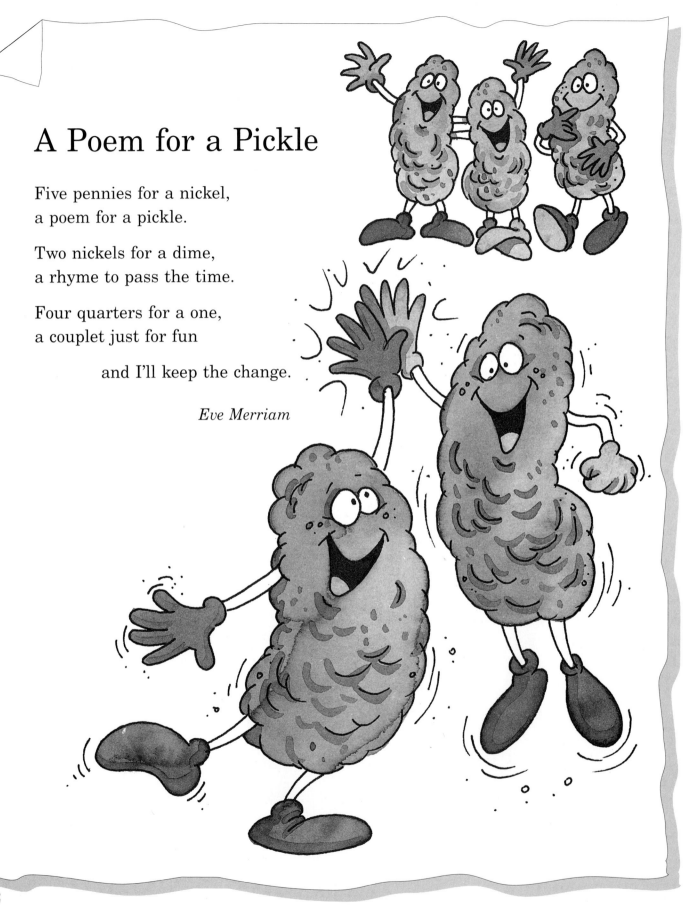

A Poem for a Pickle

Five pennies for a nickel,
a poem for a pickle.

Two nickels for a dime,
a rhyme to pass the time.

Four quarters for a one,
a couplet just for fun

      and I'll keep the change.

Eve Merriam

The Animal Store

If I had a hundred dollars to spend,
    Or maybe a little more,
I'd hurry as fast as my legs would go
    Straight to the animal store.

I wouldn't say, "How much for this or that?"—
    "What kind of a dog is he?"
I'd buy as many as rolled an eye,
    Or wagged a tail at me!

I might buy a parrot all red and green,
    And the monkey I saw before,
If I had a hundred dollars to spend,
    Or maybe a little more.

Rachel Field

Money's Funny

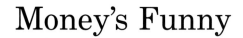

Money's funny,
Don't you think?
Nickel's bigger than a dime;
So's a cent;
But when they're spent,
Dime is worth more
Every time.

Money's funny.

Mary Ann Hoberman

Smart

My dad gave me one dollar bill
'Cause I'm his smartest son,
And I swapped it for two shiny quarters
'Cause two is more than one!

And then I took the quarters
And traded them to Lou
For three dimes—I guess he don't know
That three is more than two!

Just then, along came old blind Bates
And just 'cause he can't see
He gave me four nickels for my three dimes,
And four is more than three!

And I took the nickels to Hiram Coombs
Down at the seed-feed store,
And the fool gave me five pennies for them,
And five is more than four!

And then I went and showed my dad,
And he got red in the cheeks
And closed his eyes and shook his head—
Too proud of me to speak!

Shel Silverstein

Three Balls

A little ball,

A bigger ball,

A great big ball you see.

Let's count the balls

That we have made;

One,

Two,

Three.

Learning

This is high, and this is low,
Only see how much I know.

This is narrow, this is wide,
Something else I know besides.

Up is where the birds fly free,
Down is where my feet should be.

This is my right hand, as you see,
This is my left hand, all agree.

Overhead I raise them high,
Clap 1, 2, 3, and let them fly.

Triangle

Here's a triangle. *(spread index and middle fingers apart; right index finger forms base)*
Here's a triangle. *(draw a small triangle in the air)*
Now draw one more with me. *(draw in the air)*
Can you count them?
Are you ready?   One! *(repeat first action)*
　　　　　　　　Two! *(repeat second action)*
　　　　　　　　Three! *(repeat third action)*

Rectangle

Here's a rectangle, straight and tall: *(arms straight up, over head, fingers touch)*
Two long sides, and that's not all.
Two short sides that face each other.
Draw one rectangle, now another. *(draw in the air)*

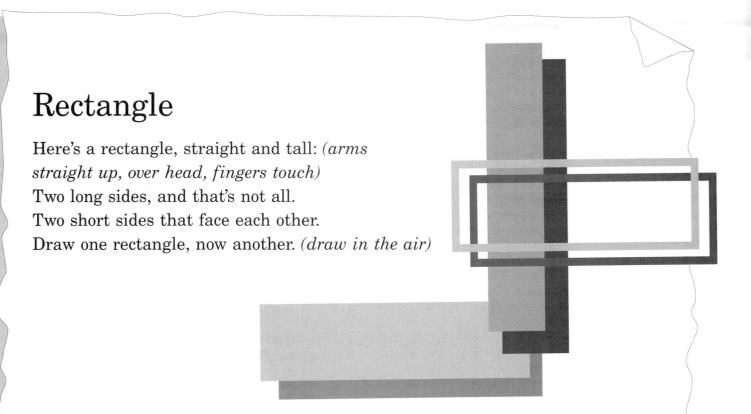

Hippity-Hop

Hippity-hop to the grocery store
To buy three sticks of candy.
One for you and one for me,
And one for sister Mandy.

Sharing

One for me & one for you
If there's one left over then what'll we do?
Take up a knife & cut it in two
So there's one for me & one for you

Clyde Watson

STORIES

...Can't I just finish the story
I'm reading here in my book?...

From "Bedtime"
by Eleanor Farjeon
page 27

A Lost Button

BY ARNOLD LOBEL

Toad and Frog went for a long walk. They walked across a large meadow. They walked in the woods. They walked along the river. At last they went back home to Toad's house.

"Oh, drat," said Toad. "Not only do my feet hurt, but I have lost one of the buttons on my jacket."

"Don't worry," said Frog. "We will go back to all the places where we walked.

We will soon find your button." They walked back to the large meadow. They began to look for the button in the tall grass.

"Here is your button!" cried Frog.

"That is not my button," said Toad. "That button is black. My button was white." Toad put the black button in his pocket.

A sparrow flew down. "Excuse me," said the sparrow. "Did you lose a button? I found one."

"That is not my button," said Toad. "That button has two holes. My button had four holes." Toad put the button with two holes in his pocket.

They went back to the woods and looked on the dark paths. "Here is your button," said Frog.

"That is not my button," cried Toad. "That button is small. My button was big." Toad put the small button in his pocket.

A raccoon came out from behind a tree. "I heard that you were looking for a button," he said. "Here is one that I just found."

"That is not my button!" wailed Toad. "That button is square. My button was round." Toad put the square button in his pocket.

Frog and Toad went back to the river. They looked for the button in the mud. "Here is your button," said Frog.

"That is not my button!" shouted Toad. "That button is thin. My button was thick." Toad put the thin button in his pocket. He was very angry. He jumped up and down and screamed, "The whole world is covered with buttons, and not one of them is mine!"

Toad ran home and slammed the door. There, on the floor, he saw his white, four-holed, big, round, thick button. "Oh," said Toad. "It was here all the time. What a lot of trouble I have made for Frog."

Toad took all of the buttons out of his pocket. He took his sewing box down from the shelf. Toad sewed the buttons all over his jacket.

The next day Toad gave his jacket to Frog. Frog thought that it was beautiful. He put it on and jumped for joy. None of the buttons fell off. Toad had sewed them on very well.

Caps for Sale

BY ESPHYR SLOBODKINA

A Tale of a Peddler, Some Monkeys
and Their Monkey Business

Once there was a peddler who sold
caps. But he was not like an ordinary
peddler carrying his wares on his back.
He carried them on top of his head.

First he had on his own checked cap,
then a bunch of gray caps, then a bunch
of brown caps, then a bunch of blue
caps, and on the very top a bunch of
red caps.

He walked up and down the streets,
holding himself very straight so as not
to upset his caps.

As he went along he called, "Caps!
Caps for sale! Fifty cents a cap!"

One morning he couldn't sell any
caps. He walked up the street and he
walked down the street calling, "Caps!
Caps for sale. Fifty cents a cap."

But nobody wanted any caps that
morning. Nobody wanted even a red cap.

He began to feel very hungry, but he
had no money for lunch.

"I think I'll go for a walk in the
country," said he. And he walked out of
town—slowly, slowly, so as not to upset
his caps.

He walked for a long time until he
came to a great big tree.

"That's a nice place for a rest,"
thought he.

And he sat down very slowly, under
the tree and leaned back little by little
against the tree-trunk so as not to
disturb the caps on his head.

Then he put up his hand to feel if
they were straight—first his own
checked cap, then the gray caps, then
the brown caps, then the blue caps, then
the red caps on the very top.

They were all there.

So he went to sleep.

He slept for a long time.

When he woke up he was refreshed
and rested.

But before standing up he felt with
his hand to make sure his caps were in
the right place.

All he felt was his own checked cap!

He looked to the right of him. No caps.

He looked to the left of him. No caps.

He looked in back of him. No caps.

He looked behind the tree. No caps.

Then he looked up into the tree. And what do you think he saw?

On every branch sat a monkey. On every monkey was a gray, or a brown, or a blue, or a red cap!

The peddler looked at the monkeys.

The monkeys looked at the peddler.

He didn't know what to do.

Finally he spoke to them.

"You monkeys, you," he said, shaking a finger at them, "you give me back my caps."

But the monkeys only shook their fingers back at him and said, "Tsz, tsz, tsz."

This made the peddler angry, so he shook both hands at them and said, "You monkeys, you! You give me back my caps."

But the monkeys only shook both their hands back at him and said, "Tsz, tsz, tsz."

Now he felt quite angry. He stamped his foot, and he said, "You monkeys, you! You better give me back my caps!"

But the monkeys only stamped their feet back at him and said, "Tsz, tsz, tsz."

By this time the peddler was really very, very angry. He stamped both his feet and shouted, "You monkeys, you! You must give me back my caps!"

But the monkeys only stamped both their feet back at him and said, "Tsz, tsz, tsz."

At last he became so angry that he pulled off his own cap, threw it on the ground, and began to walk away.

But then, each monkey pulled off his cap . . .

    and all the gray caps,

    and all the brown caps,

    and all the blue caps,

    and all the red caps came flying down out of the tree.

So the peddler picked up his caps and put them back on his head—

    first his own checked cap.

    then the gray caps,

    then the brown caps,

    then the blue caps,

    then the red caps on the very top.

And slowly, slowly, he walked back to town calling, "Caps! Caps for sale! Fifty cents a cap!"

The Three Billy-Goats Gruff

BY P. C. ASBJÖRNSEN

Once upon a time there were three billy-goats, who wanted to go up to the hillside to make themselves fat, and the name of all three was Gruff.

On the way up was a bridge over a mountain stream they had to cross; and under the bridge lived a great ugly Troll, with eyes as big as saucers, and a nose as long as a poker.

The first to cross the bridge was the youngest billy-goat Gruff.

"Trip, trap; trip, trap!" went the bridge.

"Who's that tripping over my bridge?" roared the Troll.

"Oh! It is only I, the tiniest billy-goat Gruff; and I'm going up to the hillside to make myself fat," said the billy-goat with such a small voice.

"Well, I'm coming to gobble you up," said the Troll.

"Oh, no! Please don't gobble me up. I'm too little, that I am," said the billy-goat. "Wait a bit till the second billy-goat Gruff comes. He's much bigger."

"Well! Be off with you," said the Troll.

A little while later the second billy-goat Gruff came to cross the bridge.

"Trip, trap! Trip, trap! Trip, trap!" went the bridge.

"Who's that tripping over my bridge?" roared the Troll.

"Oh! It's I, the second billy-goat Gruff, and I'm going up to the hillside to make myself fat," said the billy-goat, who hadn't such a small voice.

"Well, I'm coming to gobble you up," said the Troll.

"Oh, no! Please don't gobble me up. Wait a little till the big billy-goat Gruff comes. He's much bigger."

"Very well! Be off with you," said the Troll.

But just then up came the big billy-goat Gruff.

"Trip, trap! Trip, trap! Trip, trap!" went the bridge, for the billy-goat was so heavy that the bridge creaked and groaned under him.

"Who's that tramping over my bridge?" roared the Troll.

"It's I! The big billy-goat Gruff," said the billy-goat, who had an ugly, hoarse voice of his own.

"Well, I'm coming to gobble you up," roared the Troll.

"Well, come along! I've got two spears,
And I'll poke your nose and pierce your ears;
I've got besides two curling-stones,
And I'll bruise your body and rattle your bones."

That was what the big billy-goat said; and then he flew at the Troll and tossed him into the water. And the third billy-goat Gruff went up to the hillside. There the billy-goats got so fat they were scarcely able to walk home again; and if the fat hasn't fallen off them, why they're still fat, and so:

Snip, snap, snout,
This tale's told out.

Six Foolish Fishermen

BY BENJAMIN ELKIN

Once there were six brothers who decided to go fishing. So they went to the river and picked good spots from which to fish.

"I will sit in this boat," said the first brother.

"And I will kneel on this raft," said the second brother.

"And I will lean on this log," said the third brother.

"And I will stand on this bridge," said the fourth brother.

"And I will lie on this rock," said the fifth brother.

"And I will walk on this bank," said the sixth brother.

And that is exactly what they did.

Each brother fished from the spot he had chosen, and each one had good luck.

But when it was time to go home, the brothers became a little worried.

"We have been near the river, and over the river, and on the river," said the brother in the boat. "One of us might easily have fallen into the water and been drowned. I shall count all the brothers to be sure there are six of us."

And he began to count:

"I see one brother on the raft, That's *one*.

And another on the log. That's *two*.

And another on the bridge.
That's *three*.

And another on the rock. That's *four*.

And another on the bank. That's *five*.

"Only *five!* Woe is me. We have lost a brother!" In his sorrow he didn't even notice that he had forgotten to count himself.

"Can it really be?" cried the brother on the raft. "Has one of us been drowned, and have we really lost a brother?"

And he, too, began to count:

"I see one brother on the log.
That's *one*.

And another on the bridge. That's *two*.

And another on the rock. That's *three*.

And another on the bank. That's *four*.

And another on the boat. That's *five*.

"Only *five*. What will our dear mother say?"

And he, too, didn't even notice that he had forgotten to count himself.

"Let me check from here!" cried the brother on the log.

"I see one brother on the bridge.
That's *one*.

"And another on the rock. That's *two*.

"And another on the bank. That's *three*.

"And another in the boat. That's *four*.

"And another on the raft. That's *five*.

Five in *all,* oh, unhappy day! Why did we ever come here, for one of us to be drowned!"

Then the fourth brother counted, and the fifth and the sixth—each one counted only five brothers because each forgot to include himself.

All the brothers went back to the shore and rushed sadly up and down the river's edge, trying to see the body of their poor drowned brother.

Then along came a boy who had also been fishing, but who had not caught a single fish.

"What's the matter?" he asked. "You seem to have plenty of fish. Why do you all look so sad?"

"Because six of us came here to fish, and now there are only five of us left. One of our dear brothers has been drowned!"

The boy looked puzzled. "What do you mean, only five left? How do you figure that?"

"Look, I'll show you," said the eldest brother, and he pointed to his brothers: "One.

Two.

Three.

Four.

Five.

"Six of us came here, and now only five are going back. Sad is the day!"

The boy turned to hide his smile, and then he turned back. "I think I can help you find your lost brother," he said. "When I squeeze your hand, I want you to count."

As hard as he could, he squeezed the hand of each of the brothers, in turn.

"*One!*" yelled the first brother, and he rubbed his aching hand.

"*Two!*" cried the second brother, and he jumped up and down because of the hard squeeze.

"*Three!*" shouted the third brother.

"*Four!*" shrieked the fourth brother.

"*Five!*" screamed the fifth brother.

"*Six!*" roared the sixth brother.

"SIX!" The brothers looked at each other in delight.

There were six of them again!

They cheered for joy, and slapped each other on the back.

Gratefully, they turned to the boy. "Here," they said, "we insist that you take all of our fish. We can never thank you enough for finding our dear, lost brother."

As the boy happily accepted their gift, the six foolish fishermen went their merry way.

Counting Crocodiles

An Indonesian Tale

Once, Mouse-Deer wanted to visit his friend Monkey. Now, Monkey lived on another island, and the two of them would visit when the tide was very low—they would scamper along the sand between the two islands. But today the tide was high, and what was even worse, the water was full of crocodiles!

Mouse-Deer had an idea. He grabbed a dry leaf that looked like a crown and put it on his head. Then he stood on a high rock next to the shore.

"Listen, crocodiles!" he shouted. "Attention all crocodiles. I bring you a royal proclamation from our king. The king has declared that all crocodiles living in this sea must be counted!"

"Why does he want us to be counted?" asked an old crocodile.

"Because . . . oh . . . because he is . . . uh . . . going to invite all of you to dinner, yes, and he wants to know how much food he should prepare for you," answered Mouse-Deer.

The crocodiles looked at Mouse-Deer as if they thought he would make a fine dinner himself. But the idea of being invited to the royal palace for dinner was so wonderful that they went off to round up all their friends and relatives.

When he saw all the crocodiles swimming and thrashing in the sea before him, Mouse-Deer asked, "How shall I ever count you all? There are so many of you, and you move about so much."

Then he thought a bit and said, "Why don't you all form a long line . . . yes . . . form a long line from here, all the way to that island over there. Then I will be able to count you."

The crocodiles formed a long line, head to tail, stretching from the place where Mouse-Deer stood all the way to the island. Mouse-Deer then jumped from crocodile to crocodile, counting as he went, "One, two, three, four, five, six, seven . . . ." Then he hopped off the last crocodile and onto the island.

"You will all be receiving your dinner invitations soon!" he called out to the crocodiles. "Good-bye!"

Then Mouse-Deer trotted into the jungle to find his friend Monkey.

51

Two Ways to Count to Ten

A Liberian Folktale   RETOLD BY RUBY DEE

Long, long ago, animals were not so different, one from the other. They were different colors, shapes, and sizes just as they are today, but they lived together in friendship and in peace. The leopard was king—rich beyond telling, mighty in his power and wisdom. All the animals respected and loved their king.

"Who shall I name to rule after me when I die?" King Leopard said one day to his beloved daughter. "I must seek out the cleverest beast in our jungle. I must find one who is wise enough to rule well. I shall make him a prince. Someday, my dear daughter, the two of you shall be queen and king."

King Leopard was pleased with his idea, and he planned a great feast. His royal drums carried the news of the feast far and wide throughout the jungle.

All the animals came as guests, and they danced for three days.

At last the King told them to make a huge circle. Stepping into its center, he called his daughter to his side. Then he spoke in a loud voice.

"Listen, friends!" he cried. "Someday, when I am gone, another king must rule in my place. I will choose him now from among you so that he will be ready." There was a murmur of excitement all through the crowd.

"I shall seek the cleverest among you, for your king must be wise. He shall be a son to me and a husband to my dear daughter. He shall share all my riches."

Shouts came from the eager guests at the King's feast. No doubt each animal hoped that the good fortune would be his. Then King Leopard held up his hunting spear.

52

"Look at this, my people! Watch!" He flung the spear far up into the air and caught it when it fell to earth again. "With this spear, I will test you. He who would be our prince must also throw the spear toward the sky. He must send it so high that he can count to ten before it comes down again."

There was a buzz of talk among all the animals. This would not be so hard to do, they thought. One after another they came forward to try their skill. But first, each beast danced and sang before the King and his daughter.

"I will be first," said the elephant, pushing all the other beasts out of the way. The elephant danced clumsily. He was very big and his body was heavy. With his trunk in the air, he trumpeted all the fine deeds he would perform if he were king. "I will be king. I can do this thing!" he said. With his trunk, the great beast threw King Leopard's spear into the air.

"One! Two! Three!" he began counting.

But before the elephant had said "Four!," the King's spear dropped to the earth. The proud beast hung his head so low that the tip of his trunk dragged on the ground. He had failed.

Next came the bush ox. "I will be king. I can do this thing!" said the huge animal as he danced. "I'll throw the spear to the sun!" The bush ox picked up the spear in his mouth. With a mighty toss of his great head, he flung it far, far above his wide, gray horns.

"One! Two! Three! Four!" the bush ox counted. But he, too, was slow. Before he could say "Five!," the spear was down on

53

the ground, and he went off, ashamed, into the jungle.

The chimpanzee was third. He jumped up and down, beating his hairy chest with his fists and singing of how much he would like to be king.

The chimpanzee rose up on his hind legs and held the spear in one hand, just like a man. "I will be king. I can do this thing!" he said. With a twist of his long arm, he threw it up toward the sky. "One-two-three-four-five-six-seven!" he chattered as fast as he could. The animals held their breath. Surely, with such a quick tongue he would make the count.

But he did not! Just as he said "Eight!" the spear fell into his hand.

Then the crowd parted as the lion stepped majestically into the center of the circle. The lion had always wanted to be king anyway, and now was his chance to prove that *he* was the finest animal in the jungle. With a fling of his mighty mane, he danced and sang of his royal intentions. "*I* will be king. I can do this thing!" he sang.

And as the other animals looked on in awe, the lion twirled his tail around the spear and threw it skyward with a thunderous roar. "One! Two! Three! Four!" The spear rose higher and higher. "Five! Six! Seven! Eight! Nine!"

Just as he said "Nine!" the spear pierced the earth at his feet. The lion was furious. Off he stomped into the bushes.

One by one the other animals tried to count to ten while the spear was still in the air. One by one they all failed.

"It seems I must look somewhere else for a beast who is clever enough to rule

when I am gone," King Leopard said sadly.

"Let me try to throw your spear, O King," came a brave voice from the crowd and out stepped the slender antelope. "I would like to marry your beautiful daughter. I will be king. I can do this thing!"

"Ho! Ho! Ho! Hah! Hah! Hah!" The other animals broke into laughter. How could this weak and puny creature possibly throw the King's spear high enough to count to more than two or three? How could he hope to succeed where all the other animals—even the lion—had failed?

But the young antelope would not be turned aside. "I wish to try," he insisted. King Leopard nodded his head.

"Who can say what any creature can do until he has tried?" the King said to the crowd. "The antelope may throw the spear."

So, the other animals moved back to give him room. When the antelope danced, King Leopard's daughter was very pleased. No one could deny that his steps were more graceful than all the other animals' steps.

With a toss of his head, he flung the spear far up into the air. Before it could fall to earth, he called out five words.

"Two! Four! Six! Eight! Ten!" he cried. "I have counted to ten. King Leopard did not say how the count was to be made."

The King laughed and nodded his royal head. "No, I did not say how the count was to be made," he agreed. "And as everyone knows, one can count to ten by twos as well as by ones. Remember, my friends, it is not always the biggest or the strongest, but sometimes the cleverest that wins the prize. The antelope has won the contest. He shall be king."

At the wedding feast which King Leopard gave for his daughter, the animals all cheered their clever new prince.

How Many Spots Does A Leopard Have?

An African Tale   BY JULIUS LESTER

One morning Leopard was doing what he enjoyed doing most. He was looking at his reflection in the lake. How handsome he was! How magnificent was his coat! And, ah! The spots on his coat! Was there anything in creation more superb?

Leopard's rapture was broken when the water in the lake began moving. Suddenly Crocodile's ugly head appeared above the surface.

Leopard jumped back. Not that he was afraid. Crocodile would not bother him. But then again, one could never be too sure about Crocodile.

"Good morning, Leopard," Crocodile said. "Looking at yourself again, I see. You are the most vain creature in all of creation."

Leopard was not embarrassed. "If you were as handsome as I am, if you had such beautiful spots, you, too, would be vain."

"Spots! Who needs spots? You're probably so in love with your spots that you spend all your time counting them."

Now there was an idea that had not occurred to Leopard. "What a wonderful idea!" he exclaimed. "I would very much like to know how many spots I have." He stopped. "But there are far too many for me to count myself."

The truth was that Leopard didn't know how to count. "Perhaps you will count them for me, Crocodile?"

"Not on your life!" answered Crocodile. "I have better things to do than count spots." He slapped his tail angrily and dove beneath the water.

Leopard chuckled. "Crocodile doesn't know how to count, either."

Leopard walked along the lakeshore until he met Weasel. "Good morning, Weasel. Would you count my spots for me?"

"Who? Me? Count? Sure. One-two-three-four."

"Great!" exclaimed Leopard. "You can count."

Weasel shook his head. "But I can't. What made you think that I could?"

"But you just did. You said, 'One-two-three-four.' That's counting."

Weasel shook his head again. "Counting is much more difficult than that. There is something that comes after four, but I don't know what it is."

"Oh," said Leopard. "I wonder who knows what comes after four."

"Well, if you ask at the lake when all the animals come to drink, you will find someone who can count."

"You are right, Weasel! And I will give a grand prize to the one who tells me how many spots I have."

"What a great idea!" Weasel agreed.

That afternoon all the animals were gathered at the lake to drink. Leopard announced that he would give a magnificent prize to the one who could count his spots.

Elephant said he should be first since he was the biggest and the oldest.

"One-two-three-four-five-six-seven-eight-nine-ten," Elephant said very loudly and with great speed. He took a deep breath and began again. "One-two-three-four-five-si—"

"No! No! No!" the other animals interrupted. "You've already counted to ten once."

Elephant looked down his long trunk at the other animals. "I beg your pardon. I would appreciate it if you would not interrupt me when I am counting. You made me forget where I was. Now, where was I? I know I was somewhere in the second ten."

"The second ten?" asked Antelope. "What's that?"

"The numbers that come after the first ten, of course. I don't much care for those 'teen' things, thirteen, fourteen, and what have you. It is eminently more sensible to count ten twice and that makes twenty. That is multiplication."

None of the other animals knew what Elephant was talking about.

"Why don't you start over again?" suggested Cow.

Elephant began again and he counted ten twice and stopped. He frowned and looked very confused. Finally he said, "Leopard has more than twenty spots."

"How many more than twenty?" Leopard wanted to know.

Elephant frowned more. "A lot." Then he brightened. "In fact, you have so many more spots than twenty that I simply don't have time to count them now. I have an important engagement I mustn't be late for." Elephant started to walk away.

"Ha! Ha! Ha!" laughed Mule. "I bet Elephant doesn't know how to count higher than twenty."

Mule was right.

"Can *you* count above twenty?" Leopard asked Mule.

"Who? Me? I can only count to four because that's how many legs I have."

Leopard sighed. "Can *anyone* count above twenty?" he asked plaintively.

Bear said, "Well, once I counted up to fifty. Is that high enough?"

Leopard shrugged. "I don't know. It might be. Why don't you try and we will see."

Bear agreed. "I'll start at your tail. One-two-three-four-five-six . . . . Hm. Is that one spot or two spots?"

All the animals crowded around to get a close look. They argued for some time and finally agreed that it should only count as one.

"So, where was I?" asked Bear.

"Five," answered Turkey.

"It was six, you turkey," said Chicken.

"Better start again," suggested Crow.

Bear started again and got as far as eleven. "Eleven. That's a beautiful spot right there, Leopard."

"Which one?" Leopard wanted to know.

"Right there. Oh, dear. Or was it that spot there? They're both exquisite. My, my. I don't know where I left off counting. I must start again."

Bear counted as far as twenty-nine this time and then stopped suddenly. "Now, what comes after twenty-nine?"

"I believe thirty does," offered Turtle.

"That's right!" exclaimed Bear. "Now, where did I leave off?"

"You were still on the tail," offered Lion.

"Yes, but was that the twenty-ninth spot, or was it this one here?"

The animals started arguing again.

"You'd better start again," suggested Cow.

"Start what again?" asked Rabbit who had just arrived.

The animals explained to Rabbit about the difficulty they were having in counting Leopard's spots.

"Is that all?" Rabbit said. "I know the answer to that."

"You do?" all the animals, including Leopard, exclaimed at once.

"Certainly. It's really quite simple." Rabbit pointed to one of Leopard's spots. "This one is dark." He pointed to another. "This one is light. Dark, light, dark, light, dark, light." Rabbit continued in this way until he had touched all of Leopard's spots.

"It's simple," he concluded. "Leopard has only two spots—dark ones and light ones."

All the animals remarked on how smart Rabbit was, all of them, that is, except Leopard. He knew something was wrong with how Rabbit counted, but unless he learned to count for himself, he would never know what it was.

Leopard had no choice but to give Rabbit the magnificent prize.

What was it?

What else except a picture of Leopard himself!

The Enormous Turnip

BY ALEXEI TOLSTOY

Once upon a time an old man planted a little turnip and said: "Grow, grow, little turnip, grow sweet! Grow, grow, little turnip, grow strong!"

And the turnip grew up sweet and strong and big and enormous.

Then, one day, the old man went to pull it up. He pulled and pulled again, but he could not pull it up.

He called the old woman.

The old woman pulled the old man,
The old man pulled the turnip.

And they pulled and pulled again, but they could not pull it up.

So the old woman called her granddaughter.

The granddaughter pulled the old woman,
The old woman pulled the old man,
The old man pulled the turnip.

And they pulled and pulled again, but they could not pull it up.

The granddaughter called the black dog.

The black dog pulled the granddaughter,
The granddaughter pulled the old woman,
The old woman pulled the old man,
The old man pulled the turnip.

And they pulled and pulled again, but they could not pull it up.

The black dog called the cat.

The cat pulled the dog,
The dog pulled the granddaughter,
The granddaughter pulled the old woman,
The old woman pulled the old man,
The old man pulled the turnip.

And they pulled and pulled again, but still they could not pull it up.

The cat called the mouse.

The mouse pulled the cat,
The cat pulled the dog,
The dog pulled the granddaughter,
The granddaughter pulled the old woman,
The old woman pulled the old man,
The old man pulled the turnip.

And they pulled and pulled again, and up came the turnip at last.

Chicken Licken

BY P. C. ASBJÖRNSEN

One day when Chicken Licken was scratching among the leaves, an acorn fell out of a tree and struck her on the tail.

"Oh," said Chicken Licken, "the sky is falling! I am going to tell the King."

So she went along and went along until she met Henny Penny.

"Good morning, Chicken Licken, where are you going?" said Henny Penny.

"Oh, Henny Penny, the sky is falling and I am going to tell the King!"

"How do you know the sky is falling?" asked Henny Penny.

"I saw it with my own eyes, I heard it with my own ears, and a piece of it fell on my tail!" said Chicken Licken.

"Then I will go with you," said Henny Penny.

So they went along and went along until they met Cocky Locky.

"Good morning, Henny Penny and Chicken Licken," said Cocky Locky, "where are you going?"

"Oh, Cocky Locky, the sky is falling and we are going to tell the King!"

"How do you know the sky is falling?" asked Cocky Locky.

"Chicken Licken told me," said Henny Penny.

"I saw it with my own eyes, I heard it with my own ears, and a piece of it fell on my tail!" said Chicken Licken.

"Then I will go with you," said Cocky Locky, "and we will tell the King."

So they went along and went along until they met Ducky Daddles.

"Good morning, Cocky Locky, Henny Penny, and Chicken Licken," said Ducky Daddles, "where are you going?"

"Oh Ducky Daddles, the sky is falling and we are going to tell the King!"

"How do you know the sky is falling?" asked Ducky Daddles.

"Henny Penny told me," said Cocky Locky.

"Chicken Licken told me," said Henny Penny.

"I saw it with my own eyes, I heard it with my own ears, and a piece of it fell on my tail!" said Chicken Licken.

"Then I will go with you," said Ducky Daddles, "and we will tell the King."

So they went along and went along until they met Goosey Loosey.

"Good morning, Ducky Daddles, Cocky Locky, Henny Penny, and Chicken Licken," said Goosey Loosey, "where are you going?"

"Oh, Goosey Loosey, the sky is falling and we are going to tell the King!"

"How do you know the sky is falling?" asked Goosey Loosey.

"Cocky Locky told me," said Ducky Daddles.

"Henny Penny told me," said Cocky Locky.

"Chicken Licken told me," said Henny Penny.

"I saw it with my own eyes, I heard it with my own ears, and a piece of it fell on my tail!" said Chicken Licken.

"Then I will go with you," said Goosey Loosey, "and we will tell the King!"

So they went along and went along until they met Turkey Lurkey.

"Good morning, Goosey Loosey, Ducky Daddles, Cocky Locky, Henny Penny, and Chicken Licken," said Turkey Lurkey, "where are you going?"

"Oh, Turkey Lurkey, the sky is falling and we are going to tell the King!"

"How do you know the sky is falling?" asked Turkey Lurkey.

"Ducky Daddles told me," said Goosey Loosey.

"Cocky Locky told me," said Ducky Daddles.

"Henny Penny told me," said Cocky Locky.

"Chicken Licken told me," said Henny Penny.

"I saw it with my own eyes, I heard it with my own ears, and a piece of it fell on my tail!" said Chicken Licken.

"Then I will go with you," said Turkey Lurkey, "and we will tell the King!"

So they went along and went along until they met Foxy Woxy.

"Good morning, Turkey Lurkey, Goosey Loosey, Ducky Daddles, Cocky Locky, Henny Penny, and Chicken Licken," said Foxy Woxy, "where are you going?"

"Oh, Foxy Woxy, the sky is falling and we are going to tell the King!"

"How do you know the sky is falling?" asked Foxy Woxy.

"Goosey Loosey told me," said Turkey Lurkey.

"Ducky Daddles told me," said Goosey Loosey.

"Cocky Locky told me," said Ducky Daddles.

"Henny Penny told me," said Cocky Locky.

"Chicken Licken told me," said Henny Penny.

"I saw it with my own eyes, I heard it with my own ears, and a piece of it fell on my tail," said Chicken Licken.

"Then we will run, we will run to my den," said Foxy Woxy, "and I will tell the King."

So they all ran to Foxy Woxy's den, and the King was never told that the sky was falling.

Peace and Quiet

A YIDDISH TALE

Once, a man lived all alone in a little house. He had a good farm with cows and horses, pigs and chickens. But he was very unhappy because he could never, ever get any peace and quiet. The door in his little house creaked. The floorboards next to his little bed squeaked, and the windows rattled all night long.

With all that creaking and squeaking and rattling, the man could never even get a good night's sleep. So he went to see the wise woman. The wise woman listened to his story and thought for a while, and then asked, "Do you have a chicken?"

"Yes, I have many chickens," the man answered.

"Tonight, bring a chicken into the house," advised the wise woman.

The man went home and took a chicken into his little house. That night, the door creaked, the floorboards squeaked, the windows rattled, and the chicken cackled. The man got even less sleep than before!

So the next day, he went once again to see the wise woman. "Oh, Wise Woman," he moaned, "I did what you told me. I took a chicken into my house, and now the noise is worse than before."

The wise woman listened and nodded, and thought for a while, and then she asked, "Do you have a pig?"

"Yes," answered the man, "I have many pigs."

"Tonight, bring a pig into the house," said the wise woman.

The man went home and took a pig into his little house. That night, the door creaked, the floorboards squeaked, the windows rattled, the chicken cackled, and the pig grunted. The man lay awake the whole night with his eyes open.

The next day, he went once again to see the wise woman. "Wise Woman!" he cried. "I did what you told me. I took a pig into my house. The noise is now unbearable!"

The wise woman listened, and thought for a while, and then she asked, "Do you have a cow?"

"Yes," the man answered, "I have several cows."

"Tonight," advised the wise woman, "bring a cow into the house."

The man went home and took a cow into his little house. That night, the door creaked, the floorboards squeaked, the windows rattled, the chicken cackled, the pig grunted, and the cow mooed. The man spent the whole night sitting on the edge of his bed, holding his ears and moaning.

The next day, he went once again to see the wise woman. "Wise Woman," he whimpered, "I did what you told me. I took a cow into my house. Now I can no longer sleep. How can a man live if he does not sleep?"

The wise woman listened, and thought for a while, and looked at the man, and asked, "Do you have a horse?"

"I know, I know," said the man, and he returned home.

That night, the man took a horse into his little house. He lay down on the bed and listened. The door creaked, the floorboards squeaked, the windows rattled, the chicken cackled, the pig grunted, the cow mooed, and the horse whinnied, and the man got up, got dressed, and ran to the house of the wise woman.

"Wise Woman! Wise Woman!" cried the man. "Help me!"

"I think," said the wise woman, "that it is time to kick all those noisy animals out of your house."

Wearily, the man trudged home, and happily he put the horse, the cow, the pig, and the chicken back in the barn where they belonged. Then he lay down and fell asleep. The door creaked, but he did not wake up. The floorboards squeaked, but he did not wake up. The windows rattled, but he did not wake up. He slept soundly and peacefully until morning.

"At last," he sighed. "Peace and quiet!"

The Three Bears

Once upon a time there were three bears: a great, big Papa Bear, a middle-sized Mama Bear, and a wee, little Baby Bear. The three bears lived in a cottage near the woods. Each of the bears had a bowl for porridge. There was a wee, little bowl for the wee, little Baby Bear, a middle-sized bowl for the middle-sized Mama Bear, and a great, big bowl for the great, big Papa Bear.

They had chairs of their own, too. There was a wee, little chair for the wee, little Baby Bear, a middle-sized chair for the middle-sized Mama Bear, and a great, big chair for the great, big Papa Bear.

Each bear also had a bed to sleep in. There was a wee, little bed for the wee, little Baby Bear, a middle-sized bed for the middle-sized Mama Bear, and a great, big bed for the great, big Papa Bear.

One morning, the three bears decided to take a walk before breakfast because their porridge was too hot to eat. While the bears were out walking, a little girl named Goldilocks came by their house and peeked in the window. She saw that no one was at home, so she opened the door and walked right in.

Goldilocks saw the three bowls of porridge cooling on the table. She

decided that she would taste the porridge, and that she did. First, she tasted the great, big Papa Bear's great, big bowl of porridge. It was much too hot for Goldilocks to eat. Next, she tasted the middle-sized Mama Bear's middle-sized bowl of porridge. It was too cold for Goldilocks to eat. Last, she tasted the wee, little Baby Bear's bowl of porridge. It was just right. Goldilocks liked it so much that she gobbled up every bit of the Baby Bear's porridge.

Then Goldilocks saw the three chairs in the living room. First, she sat in the great, big Papa Bear's great, big chair, but it was much too hard. Next, she sat in the middle-sized Mama Bear's middle-sized chair, but it was too soft for

Goldilocks. Last, she sat in the wee, little Baby Bear's wee, little chair. It was just right, so she rocked and she rocked and she rocked in the little chair until . . . she rocked so hard that the chair broke and Goldilocks fell out of the chair.

Next, Goldilocks went upstairs to see what she could find. She went into the three bears' bedroom and saw the three beds. First, she tried the great, big Papa Bear's great, big bed but it was too high for Goldilocks. Next, she tried the middle-sized Mama Bear's middle-sized bed but it was too low for Goldilocks. Last, she tried the wee, little Baby Bear's wee, little bed. It was just right. It was so comfortable that Goldilocks lay right there until she fell sound asleep.

Soon, the three bears came home from their morning walk. They saw right away that someone had been in their home. Papa Bear looked at his great, big bowl of porridge and roared in his great, big voice, "SOMEONE HAS BEEN EATING MY PORRIDGE!"

Mama Bear looked at her middle-sized bowl of porridge and said in her middle-sized voice, "Someone has been eating my porridge!"

Baby Bear looked at his wee, little bowl of porridge and cried in his wee, little voice, "Someone has been eating my porridge and has eaten it all up!"

Then the bears went into the living room and saw their chairs. Papa Bear looked at his great, big chair and roared

in his great, big voice, "SOMEONE HAS BEEN SITTING IN MY CHAIR!"

Mama Bear looked at her middle-sized chair and said in her middle-sized voice, "Someone has been sitting in my chair!"

Baby Bear looked at his wee, little broken chair and cried in his wee, little voice, "Someone has been sitting in my chair and has broken it all to bits!"

The three bears decided that they should look upstairs. Up the stairs and into their bedroom they went. Papa Bear looked at his great, big bed and roared in his great, big voice, "SOMEONE HAS BEEN LYING IN MY BED!"

Mama Bear looked at her middle-sized bed and said in her middle-sized voice, "Someone has been lying in my bed!"

Baby Bear looked at his wee, little bed and cried in his wee, little voice, "Someone has been lying in my bed and here she is!"

At that moment, Goldilocks woke up. When she opened her eyes and saw the three bears looking down at her, she jumped up and ran out of the cottage as fast as she could go. The three bears never saw Goldilocks again. They lived happily ever after in their cottage near the woods.

6 O'Clock Rooster

BY MELVERN BARKER

On a little farm in the country lived a family of four: a mother, a father, a little boy, and a cat named Mooch. Every morning very early they all awoke when the rooster crowed.

The father had his work to do.
The mother had her work to do.
The little boy did chores.

They were happy country people.

There was also a family of four who lived in the city.
A father who had his work to do.
A mother who had many things to do.

A little boy who ran errands and a little dog named Pooch who just slept.

Every morning very early they all awoke when the street noises began. They were happy city people.

The country boy and the city boy were cousins. One day the country boy wrote a letter to his city cousin. It said, "Please come and visit me and I will show you how we live in the country."

The city cousin wrote back and said, "I will come; I want to know about the country."

When the city boy arrived they all had a big country supper. Then the two cousins went to bed in a big country bed.

The little country boy fell fast asleep right away. But the little city boy did not, for he heard all kinds of strange noises which kept him awake.

The wind whistled in the trees, the crickets chirped, the gate creaked, the windmill banged, and just as the sun was coming up he heard the loudest noise of all—the rooster crowed. He seemed to say, "Get up, get up, for this is a beautiful day."

Then all was very quiet and the city boy finally got to sleep. He slept until ten o'clock.

When he awoke he thought, "I wish I could be a country boy and get up when everyone else does."

At breakfast the country boy's mother said, "I am glad to see you, but what made you sleep so long?"

"All the noises kept me awake," said the city boy. "And I could not sleep until they stopped early in the morning."

72

"What noises do you mean?" asked the mother.

The city boy said, "I heard the wind, I heard something chirp, I heard a creaking noise, I heard a bang, and then I heard a very loud funny noise early in the morning. Then all was quiet and I fell asleep."

"Why, those are country noises," said the country boy's mother, "and soon you will be used to them. Now go out and help feed the pigs."

So the city boy joined the country boy and they fed the pigs.

The second night the little city boy went to bed very tired. Again he heard the wind whistle, the gate creak, the crickets chirp, and at daybreak the rooster crowed.

When the rooster stopped crowing he went to sleep and slept until nine o'clock. He got up and had his breakfast. He helped feed the pigs and chickens.

The third night he heard the wind whistle, the gate creak, the crickets chirp, but the noises didn't seem so loud. He went to sleep and slept until the sun came up and the rooster crowed, "Get up, get up." But he didn't get up until eight o'clock. Then he had his breakfast and helped feed the pigs, the chickens, and the calf.

The fourth night he hardly heard the noises at all. When the sun came up and the rooster crowed he only stayed in bed until seven o'clock. He had his breakfast and helped feed the pigs, the chickens, the calf, and the colt.

The fifth night he went to bed and heard no noise at all. He fell asleep and slept the whole night through.

So when the sun came up and the rooster crowed, the little city boy got right up at six o'clock. He had a big country breakfast with all his country cousins.

"The noises have stopped," he said.

Everyone laughed. "The noises haven't stopped," said the country boy's mother, "for last night the wind whistled, the crickets chirped, the gate creaked, and the windmill banged."

"You've just got used to the country noises," said the country boy. "You get up with the six o'clock rooster; so now you're a country boy, too."

Very Tall Mouse and Very Short Mouse

BY ARNOLD LOBEL

Once there was a very tall mouse and a very short mouse who were good friends. When they met Very Tall Mouse would say, "Hello, Very Short Mouse."

And Very Short Mouse would say, "Hello, Very Tall Mouse."

The two friends would often take walks together. As they walked along Very Tall Mouse would say, "Hello birds."

And Very Short Mouse would say, "Hello bugs."

When they passed by a garden Very Tall Mouse would say, "Hello flowers."

And Very Short Mouse would say, "Hello roots."

When they passed by a house Very Tall Mouse would say, "Hello roof."

And Very Short Mouse would say, "Hello cellar."

One day the two mice were caught in a storm. Very Tall Mouse said, "Hello raindrops."

And Very Short Mouse said, "Hello puddles."

They ran indoors to get dry. "Hello ceiling," said Very Tall Mouse.

"Hello floor," said Very Short Mouse.

Soon the storm was over. The two friends ran to the window. Very Tall Mouse held Very Short Mouse up to see. "Hello rainbow!" they both said together.

How Big Is A Foot?

BY ROLF MYLLER

Once upon a time there lived a King and his wife, the Queen. They were a happy couple for they had everything in the World.

However . . . when the Queen's birthday came near the King had a problem: What could he give to Someone who had Everything?

The King thought and he thought and he thought. Until suddenly, he had an idea! HE WOULD GIVE THE QUEEN A BED.

The Queen did not have a bed because at the time beds had not been invented. So even Someone who had Everything—did not have a bed.

The King called his Prime Minister and asked him to please have a bed made. The Prime Minister called the Chief Carpenter and asked him to please have a bed made. The Chief Carpenter called the apprentice and told him to make a bed.

"How big is a bed?" asked the apprentice, who didn't know because at the time nobody had ever seen a bed. "How big is a bed?" the Carpenter asked the Prime Minister. "A good question," said the Prime Minister. And he asked the King, "HOW BIG *IS* A BED?"

The King thought and he thought and he thought. Until suddenly he had an idea! THE BED MUST BE BIG ENOUGH TO FIT THE QUEEN.

The King called the Queen. He told her to put on her new pajamas and told her to lie on the floor.

The King took off his shoes and with his big feet walked carefully around the Queen. He counted that the bed must be

THREE FEET WIDE

AND

SIX FEET LONG

to be big enough to fit the Queen. (Including the crown which the Queen sometimes liked to wear to sleep.)

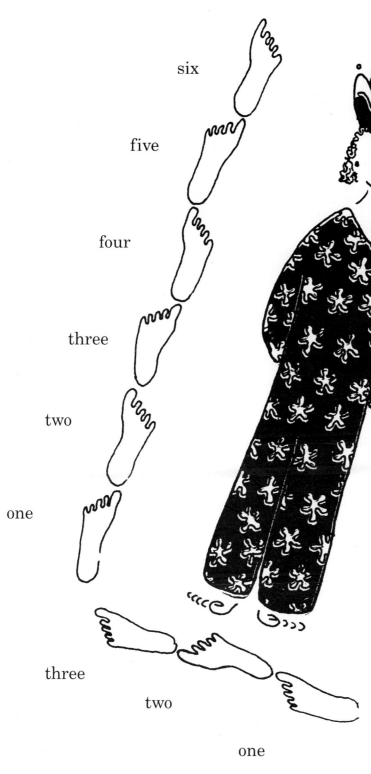

six

five

four

three

two

one

three

two

one

The King said, "Thank you," to the Queen, and told the Prime Minister, who told the Chief Carpenter, who told the apprentice: "The bed must be three feet wide and six feet long to be big enough to fit the Queen." (Including the crown which she sometimes liked to wear to sleep.)

The apprentice said "Thank you," and took off his shoes, and with his little feet he measured three feet wide and six feet long and made a bed to fit the Queen.

When the King saw the bed, he thought it was beautiful. He could not wait for the Queen's Birthday.

Instead, he called the Queen at once and told her to put on her new pajamas. Then he brought out the bed and told the queen to try it.

BUT

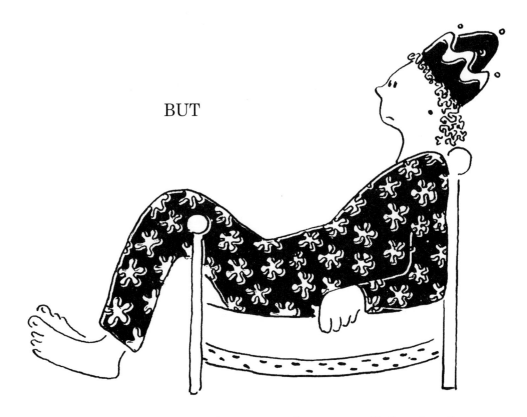

the bed was much too small for the Queen.

The King was so angry that he immediately called the Prime Minister who called the Chief Carpenter who called the jailer who threw the apprentice into jail.

The apprentice was unhappy. WHY WAS THE BED TOO SMALL FOR THE QUEEN?

He thought and he thought and he thought. Until suddenly he had an idea!

A bed that was three King's feet wide and six King's feet long was naturally bigger than a bed that was three apprentice feet wide and six apprentice feet long. "I CAN MAKE A BED TO FIT THE QUEEN IF I KNOW THE SIZE OF THE KING'S FOOT," he cried.

He explained this to the jailer, who explained it to the Chief Carpenter, who explained it to the Prime Minister, who explained it to the King, who was much too busy to go to the jail.

Instead, the King took off one shoe and called a famous sculptor. The sculptor made an exact marble copy of the King's foot. This was sent to the jail.

The apprentice took the marble copy of the King's foot, and with it he measured . . .

78

three feet wide

and six feet long and

built a bed to fit the Queen!

The Bed was ready just in time for the Queen's Birthday. The King called the Queen and told her to put on her new pajamas.

Then he brought out the New Bed and told the Queen to try it. The Queen got into bed and . . .

THE BED FIT THE QUEEN PERFECTLY. (Including the crown which she sometimes liked to wear to sleep.)

It was, without a doubt, the nicest gift that the Queen had ever received.

The King was very happy. He immediately called the apprentice from jail and made him a royal prince. He ordered a big parade, and all the people came out to cheer the little apprentice prince.

And forever after, anyone who wanted to measure anything used a copy of the King's foot. And when someone said, "My bed is six feet long and three feet wide," everyone knew exactly how big it was.

KOALA LOU

BY MEM FOX

There was once a baby koala so soft and round that all who saw her loved her. Her name was Koala Lou.

The emu loved her. The platypus loved her. And even tough little Koala Klaws next door loved her.

But it was her mother who loved her most of all. A hundred times a day she would laugh and shake her head and say, "Koala Lou, I DO love you!"

Whenever she stretched in the early morning sun, or climbed a gum tree, or bravely went down the path all by herself, her mother would smile and say, "Koala Lou, I DO love you!"

The years passed and other koalas were born—brothers and sisters for Koala Lou. Soon her mother was so busy she didn't have time to tell Koala Lou that she loved her.

Although of course she did.

Every night, as she curled up under the stars, Koala Lou thought about the times when her mother had looked at her and said, "Koala Lou, I DO love you!" and she longed for her to say it again. One night Koala Lou had a splendid idea. Preparations had begun for the Bush Olympics. SHE would enter the Olympics! She would compete in the gum tree climbing event, and she would win, and her mother would fling her arms around her neck and say again, "Koala Lou, I DO love you!"

Koala Lou began her training right away. She jogged and puffed and lifted weights and panted. She hung from a branch with one claw at a time till she ached. She did push-ups till her stomach hurt, and last of all, she climbed the tallest tree that she could find, over and over and over again.

Sometimes her mother would watch her and ask, "How're ya goin', blossom?" "Fine, just fine," Koala Lou would reply.

At last the day of the Bush Olympics arrived.

Koala Klaws had also entered the gum tree climbing event and everyone knew

how fast she was, but Koala Lou wasn't scared. She saw her mother in the crowd and imagined her saying again, "Koala Lou, I DO love you!" Her heart filled with hope.

It was Koala Klaws who went first. Her climb was a record-breaking twenty-two meters in seventy seconds flat. The spectators whistled and cheered and wildly waved their party hats.

"Can I do better than that?" wondered Koala Lou. "I must." As she stepped toward the tree, a hush fell over the crowd. "On your mark," said the kookaburra. "Get set—GO!"

Koala Lou leapt onto the tree. Up and up and up she climbed—higher and higher and higher. Faster and faster and faster until—there she was, right at the very top! The spectators roared and clapped and stamped their feet.

But she wasn't fast enough. In spite of all her training and all her hoping, it

was Koala Klaws who won the gum tree climbing. Koala Lou came second.

Koala Lou went off and hid. She heard the shouts of the Bush Olympics and cried her heart out.

When the first stars of evening appeared in the sky, Koala Lou crept home through the dark and up into the gum tree. Her mother was waiting for her. Before she could say a word, her mother had flung her arms around her neck and said, "Koala Lou, I DO love you! I always have, and I always will."

And she hugged her for a very long time.

Arthur's Funny Money

BY LILLIAN HOBAN

It was Saturday morning. Violet was counting numbers on her fingers. Arthur was counting the money in his piggy bank. He counted three dollars and seventy-eight cents. "Arthur," said Violet, "do you know numbers?"

"Yes I do," said Arthur. "I am working with numbers right now."

"Well," said Violet, "if I have five peas and you take three and give me back two, how many peas will I have?"

"All of them," said Arthur. "I don't like peas, so I wouldn't take any."

"I know you don't like peas," said Violet. "But I am trying to do a number problem. Will you help me?"

"I have my own number problem," said Arthur. He turned his piggy bank upside down and shook it. But no more money came out. "I don't have five dollars to buy a T-shirt and matching cap," said Arthur. "Everyone on our Frisbee team has to buy them. They have FAR OUT FRISBEES printed on them in blue, and they light up in the dark."

"Wilma's big sister is running errands to make money," said Violet. "She wants to buy a new catcher's mitt."

"I don't like running errands," said Arthur.

"You could wash cars," said Violet. "The junior high kids always wash cars to raise money. That's what they are doing this afternoon."

"Well, if they are washing cars, then I can't," said Arthur. "There would be too many of us in the car-wash business."

"I know!" said Violet. "You could wash bikes! Lots of kids would pay to have their bikes washed."

"Great!" said Arthur. "I could get the rust off the wheels, and I could shine up the frames. I could make lots of money."

"That's no fair," said Violet. "I told you about the bike wash. But you never told me about the peas."

"I will," said Arthur. "But first help me set up business."

Violet went into the kitchen. She got a pail and a brush. She got a cloth and a sponge. Then she took them to the back steps.

Arthur was making a sign. It said:

"There is no soap or Brillo," said Violet. "We have to buy some."

Arthur put his money in a bag and they went to the store. Arthur bought a box of soap for 53¢ and a box of Brillo for 27¢. "I hope lots of kids want their bikes washed," said Violet.

When they got home, Norman was waiting with his little brother and their dog, Bubbles. "How much is it for a tricycle?" asked Norman's little brother.

"The same as for a bike," said Arthur.

"But a trike is only half as big as a bike," said Norman.

"You should charge half as much."

"Well," said Arthur, "it's half as big, but it has more wheels."

"Tell you what," said Norman. "I will give you 38¢ for my bike and his trike. How's that for a deal?" Arthur thought about it. He opened the box of soap. He filled the pail with water. Then he counted on his fingers and thought some more.

"Look what Bubbles is doing," said Norman's little brother. Bubbles was eating the soap out of the box. And he was drinking water out of the pail.

"That's why we call him Bubbles," said Norman.

"He ate most of my soap," yelled Arthur. "You better pay me back."

"I will give you 42¢ for washing the bike and the trike," said Norman quickly. "You'll be able to buy lots of soap."

"I don't want to buy more soap," said Arthur. "I want to buy a Frisbee T-shirt and matching cap."

"Bubbles is eating Brillo for dessert," said Violet.

"Get that dog out of here!" shouted Arthur. "He's spoiling my business!"

"You have to advertise if you want business," said Norman. "Tell you what I'll do for you . . . you wash my bike and put a sign on it saying:

ARTHUR WASHED ME

I'll ride all over town and get you lots of business."

"Me too," said Norman's brother.

"It won't cost you anything," said Norman, "and you'll make lots of money."

So Arthur washed the bike and the trike. He got the rust off the wheels. And he shined up the frames. Then he made two signs, and put one on each of them. "Okay," said Norman, "we're ready to ride." He gave Arthur 42¢ and he and his little brother rode off.

Arthur put the 42¢ in the bag with the rest of his money. "You hold the money for me," he said to Violet, "and write down every time I get some. When it gets to $5.25, I'm quitting."

"What's the extra 25¢ for?" asked Violet.

"For licorice twists," said Arthur. "I just love licorice twists." He gave Violet some paper and a pencil. "Now," said Arthur, "write down $3.78. That's how much I had to start. Under that write take away 53¢, and take away 27¢. That's for the soap and Brillo." Violet wrote down all the numbers.

"Now add on 42¢," said Arthur. "And that's how much I have now."

"How much is that?" asked Violet.

"Let's see," said Arthur, and he started to count on his fingers.

"I thought you said you knew numbers," said Violet.

"I do," said Arthur. "Look! There's a parade at the corner, and it's coming this way!"

"That's not a parade," said Violet. "It's Wilma and her cousin Peter and his friend John."

Wilma was wheeling a doll buggy with a rocking horse in it, and she was pulling a stroller. Peter was driving a fire engine and pulling a wagon with a sled in it. John was riding a scooter and carrying a skateboard. "We saw the sign," said Wilma, "and we came to get washed."

"Arthur only washes bikes," said Violet.

"No I don't," said Arthur quickly, and he rolled up his sleeves. He put more water in the pail, and he put in the rest of the soap. "Wow!" said Arthur. "I'm going to clean up! This will make me lots of money!" Violet got her pencil and paper ready. Wilma's cousin Peter was whispering something to Wilma.

"Wait a minute," said Wilma. "We thought you washed for free."

"For free!" yelled Arthur. "Can't you read that sign?"

Wilma's cousin whispered to her again. "The sign on Norman's bike didn't say anything about money," said Wilma. "It's against the law to tell a lie on a sign."

"I didn't tell a lie on a sign," said Arthur. "This sign right here says bikes washed 25¢. And that's what I'm washing. No scooters or doll buggies or anything else!" Arthur pulled his sleeves down.

Peter pulled Wilma's sleeve and whispered some more. "Okay," said Wilma. "We'll go get our bikes. You can wash them for 25¢ apiece if you do the rest for free."

Arthur thought about it. He looked at the empty box of soap. He stirred the water in the pail. "Tell you what," said Arthur. "Throw in a little extra so I can buy more soap, and I will do it. How's that for a deal?"

So Wilma and Peter and John got their bikes. Arthur scrubbed the wheels and he shined the frames. He washed the buggy, the stroller, and the rocking horse for Wilma. She gave Arthur 34¢. He washed the fire engine, the sled, and the wagon for Peter. He gave Arthur 36¢. He washed the scooter and the skateboard for John. He gave Arthur 33¢.

Violet put all the money in the bag, and she wrote down all the numbers. After Wilma and Peter and John left, Arthur said, "Now let's get more soap so I can make more money."

Arthur and Violet took the bag of money and went to the store. Arthur got a box of soap and counted out 53¢. "Sorry, son," said the grocer. "This soap costs 64¢."

"But it was 53¢ this morning," said Arthur.

"That's right," said the grocer, "but the price went up. You can't get soap at this morning's price this afternoon."

"That's no fair," said Arthur.

"Maybe they still have it at this morning's price at some other store," said Violet.

Arthur and Violet went down the street. They passed the hardware store and the fruit-and-vegetable store. Then they came to the general store. There was a T-shirt and matching cap in the window. The T-shirt said FAR OUT FRISBEES on it in blue. A sign said: Window Samples Reduced

"Maybe you don't have to buy more soap to make more money," said Violet. "Maybe you have enough right now."

Arthur and Violet went into the store. "How much is the sample in the window?" asked Arthur.

"$4.25," said the saleslady. "Do you have enough money?"

"I don't know," said Arthur. "I have to count it." He poured his money out of the bag. "It will take a long time to count all that," said the lady.

"No it won't," said Violet. "Arthur knows numbers, and I have the numbers written down."

She gave Arthur the paper with the numbers on it. "Let's see," said Arthur. "$3.78, take away 53¢, take away 27¢, add 42¢, add 34¢, add 36¢, add 33¢. Hmmnnnn . . ."

"That's $4.43," said the lady. "You have enough for the T-shirt and cap, and 18¢ left over."

"Wow!" said Arthur. "I'll take the T-shirt and cap, and do you have any licorice twists?"

"Yes," said the lady. "They are 5¢ apiece or six for a quarter."

"How many do I get for 18¢?" asked Arthur.

"You'll see," said the lady. She winked at Violet.

Violet looked at Arthur. "Arthur," she said, "you said you knew numbers."

"Here are five licorice twists," said the lady. "I've given you two extra for good luck."

"Arthur," said Violet, "if I have five peas and you take three and give me back two . . ."

"Wait," said Arthur. "Change the peas to licorice twists, and I will help you."

"Okay," said Violet. "How many licorice twists will I have?"

"Hold out your hand," said Arthur. He gave Violet the five licorice twists. Then he took away three, and gave back two. "You would have four licorice twists," said Arthur. "But that only leaves me with ONE!"

"You *do* know numbers, Arthur," said Violet, and she started to eat her licorice twists. Arthur looked at the one he had left.

"I got mixed up," he said. "You would only have two."

"I know," said Violet. "Because if you took three licorice twists, you wouldn't give back any! You just love licorice twists!"

So Violet and Arthur shared the licorice twists, and they each had two and a half!

The House That Jack Built

This is the house that Jack built.

This is the malt that lay in the house that Jack built.

This is the rat, that ate the malt
   that lay in the house that Jack built.

This is the cat, that killed the rat,
   that ate the malt that lay in the house that Jack built.

This is the dog, that worried the cat,
   that killed the rat,
   that ate the malt that lay in the house that Jack built.

This is the cow with the crumpled horn,
   that tossed the dog, that worried the cat,
   that killed the rat,
   that ate the malt that lay in the house that Jack built.

This is the maiden all forlorn, that milked the cow with the
   crumpled horn, that tossed the dog,
   that worried the cat, that killed the rat,
   that ate the malt that lay in the house that Jack built.

house

rat

cow

cat

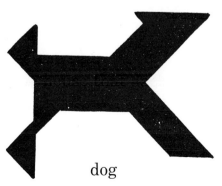

dog

This is the man all tattered and torn, that kissed the maiden
    all forlorn, that milked the cow with the crumpled horn,
    that tossed the dog, that worried the cat,
    that killed the rat,
    that ate the malt that lay in the house that Jack built.

This is the priest all shaven and shorn, that married the man
    all tattered and torn, that kissed the maiden all forlorn,
    that milked the cow with the crumpled horn,
    that tossed the dog, that worried the cat,
    that killed the rat,
    that ate the malt that lay in the house that Jack built.

This is the cock that crowed in the morn, that waked the priest
    all shaven and shorn, that married the man
    all tattered and torn, that kissed the maiden all forlorn,
    that milked the cow with the crumpled horn,
    that tossed the dog, that worried the cat,
    that killed the rat,
    that ate the malt that lay in the house that Jack built.

This is the farmer sowing his corn, that kept the cock,
    that waked the priest,
    that married the man,
    that kissed the maiden,
    that milked the cow,
    that tossed the dog,
    that worried the cat,
    that killed the rat,
    that ate the malt,
    that lay in the house that Jack built.

90

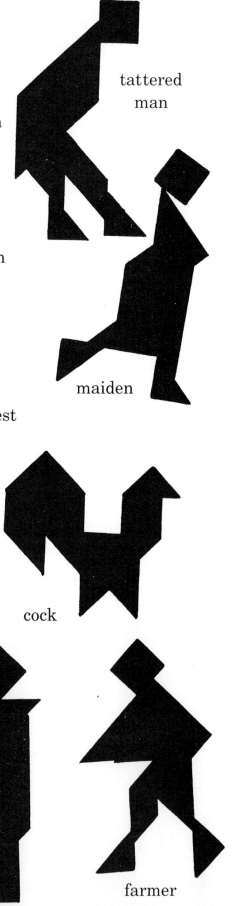

tattered
man

maiden

cock

priest

farmer

The Doorbell Rang   <small>BY PAT HUTCHINS</small>

"I've made some cookies for tea," said Ma.

"Good," said Victoria and Sam. "We're starving."

"Share them between yourselves," said Ma. "I made plenty."

"That's six each," said Sam and Victoria.

"They look as good as Grandma's," said Victoria.

"They smell as good as Grandma's," said Sam.

"No one makes cookies like Grandma," said Ma as the doorbell rang.

It was Tom and Hannah from next door.

"Come in," said Ma. "You can share the cookies."

"That's three each," said Sam and Victoria.

"They smell as good as your Grandma's," said Tom.

"And look as good," said Hannah.

"No one makes cookies like Grandma," said Ma as the doorbell rang.

It was Peter and his little brother.

"Come in," said Ma. "You can share the cookies."

"That's two each," said Victoria and Sam.

"They look as good as your Grandma's," said Peter. "And smell as good."

"Nobody makes cookies like Grandma," said Ma as the doorbell rang.

It was Joy and Simon with their four cousins.

"Come in," said Ma. "You can share the cookies."

"That's one each," said Sam and Victoria.

"They smell as good as your Grandma's," said Joy.

"And look as good," said Simon.

"No one makes cookies like Grandma," said Ma as the doorbell rang and rang.

"Oh dear," said Ma as the children stared at the cookies on their plates. "Perhaps you'd better eat them before we open the door."

"We'll wait," said Sam.

It was Grandma with an enormous tray of cookies.

"How nice to have so many friends to share them with," said Grandma. "It's a good thing I made a lot!"

"And no one makes cookies like Grandma," said Ma as the doorbell rang.

SONGS

If you listen, I'll sing you a song...

From "I'll Sing You a Song"
in *Ten Potatoes in a Pot and Other Counting Rhymes*
by *Michael Jay Katz*
page 16

Clap Your Hands

Moderately fast ♩ =108

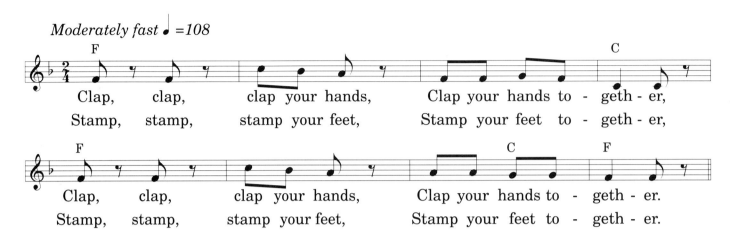

Clap, clap, clap your hands, Clap your hands to - geth - er,
Stamp, stamp, stamp your feet, Stamp your feet to - geth - er,

Clap, clap, clap your hands, Clap your hands to - geth - er.
Stamp, stamp, stamp your feet, Stamp your feet to - geth - er.

INTERLUDE (children continue rhythmic play)

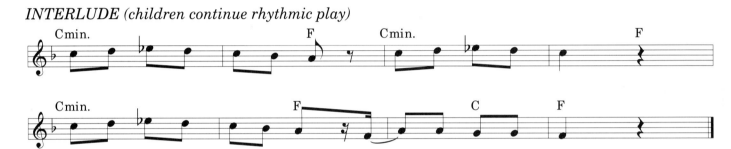

Tap, tap, tap your toes, *etc.*
Nod, nod, nod your head, *etc.*
Shake, shake, shake your hands, *etc.*
Stretch, stretch, stretch up high, *etc.*
Wheels, wheels going round, *etc.*
Dig, dig, dig the ground, *etc.*
See, see, see the moon, *etc.*
Sing, sing, sing a song, *etc.*

Loop de Loo

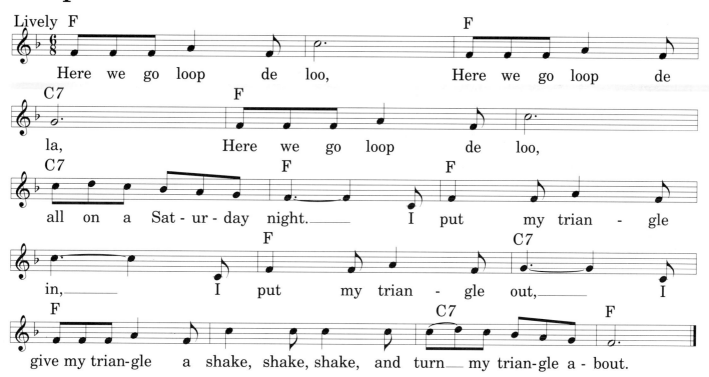

Lively

Here we go loop de loo, Here we go loop de la, Here we go loop de loo, all on a Sat-ur-day night.___ I put my trian - gle in,___ I put my trian - gle out,___ I give my trian-gle a shake, shake, shake, and turn___ my trian-gle a - bout.

I put my square in, *etc.*
I put my circle in, *etc.*
I put my rectangle in, *etc.*

Mary Mack

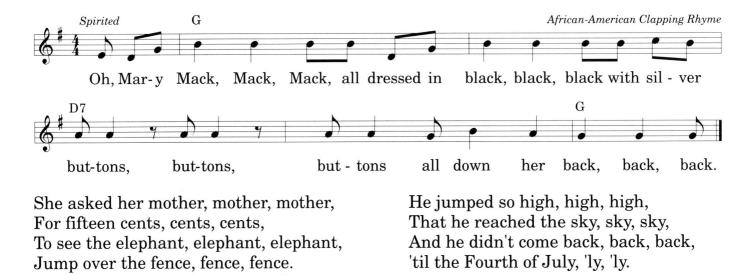

Spirited   G   *African-American Clapping Rhyme*

Oh, Mar-y Mack, Mack, Mack, all dressed in black, black, black with sil - ver but-tons, but-tons, but - tons all down her back, back, back.

She asked her mother, mother, mother,
For fifteen cents, cents, cents,
To see the elephant, elephant, elephant,
Jump over the fence, fence, fence.

He jumped so high, high, high,
That he reached the sky, sky, sky,
And he didn't come back, back, back,
'til the Fourth of July, 'ly, 'ly.

Navajo Happy Song

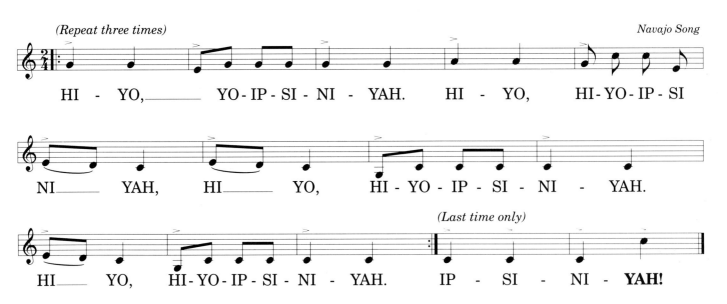

(Repeat three times)   *Navajo Song*

HI - YO, YO-IP-SI-NI-YAH. HI - YO, HI-YO-IP-SI

NI YAH, HI YO, HI-YO-IP-SI-NI-YAH.

(Last time only)

HI YO, HI-YO-IP-SI-NI-YAH. IP - SI - NI - **YAH!**

The Inch Worm

Frank Loesser

Slowly

mp

Dm — A(7) — Dm — A(7) — F/C

Two and two are four, Four and four are eight; That's all you

Bm7-5(G7) — Bbm(6) — C(7) — F — Dm — Eb(9)

have on your bus'-ness-like mind. Two and two are four,

Dm — D(7)/C — Bb(maj7) — Bbm(6) — C($^7_4$) — C(7)

Four and four are eight; How can you be so blind?

Obbligato F — Eb — F — Eb

Two and two are four, Four and four are eight,

Melody

Inch worm, inch worm, Mea-sur-ing the mar-i-golds,

1.
F — F(7) — Bb(maj7) — Bbm(6) — F/A — G(7) — C

Eight and eight are six-teen, Six-teen and six-teen are thir-ty-two.

You and your a-rith-me-tic, You'll prob-a-bly go far.

2.
F — F(7) — Bb — Bbm(6) — F/C — C(7–9) — F — Db(maj7) — F

Eight and eight are six-teen, Six-teen and six-teen are thir-ty-two.

Seems to me you'd stop and see How beau-ti-ful they are.

Mexican Counting Song

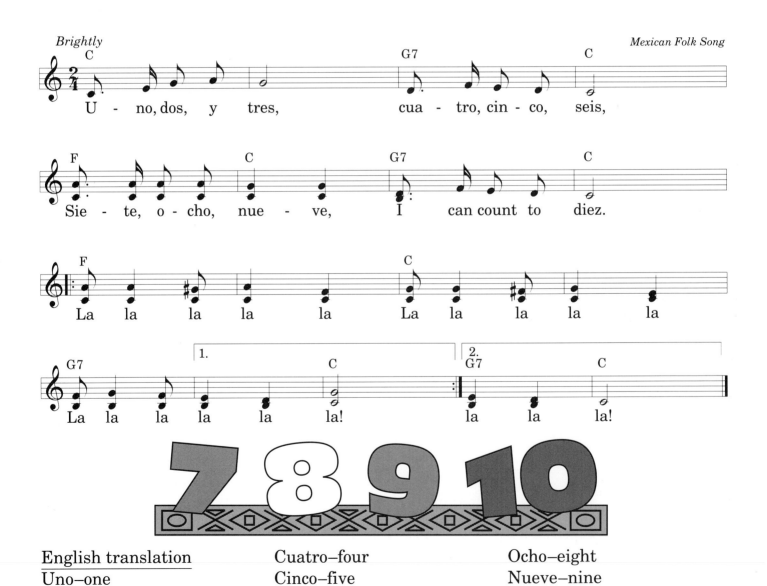

Brightly   *Mexican Folk Song*

U - no, dos, y tres, cua - tro, cin - co, seis,

Sie - te, o - cho, nue - ve, I can count to diez.

La la la la la La la la la la

La la la la la la! la la la!

English translation

Uno–one

Dos–two

Tres–three

Cuatro–four

Cinco–five

Seis–six

Siete–seven

Ocho–eight

Nueve–nine

Diez–ten

The Pattern Train

Bryan A. Fitzgerald

A Section:

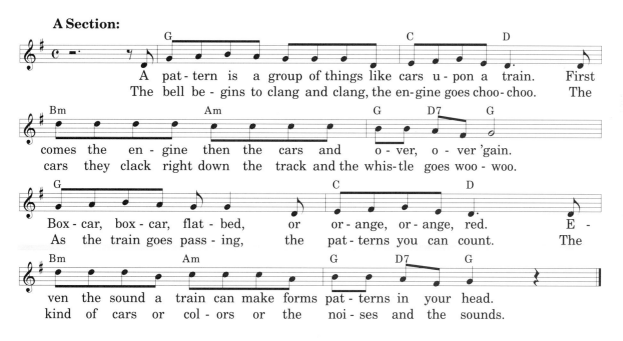

A pat - tern is a group of things like cars u - pon a train. First
The bell be - gins to clang and clang, the en - gine goes choo - choo. The

comes the en - gine then the cars and o - ver, o - ver 'gain.
cars they clack right down the track and the whis - tle goes woo - woo.

Box - car, box - car, flat - bed, or or - ange, or - ange, red. E -
As the train goes pass - ing, the pat - terns you can count. The

ven the sound a train can make forms pat - terns in your head.
kind of cars or col - ors or the noi - ses and the sounds.

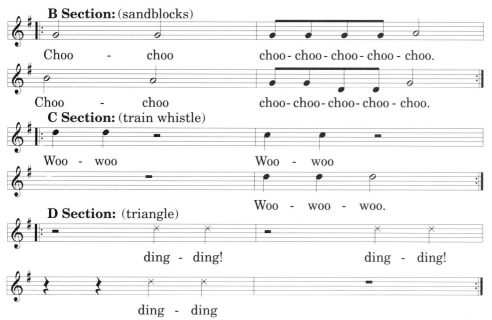

B Section: (sandblocks)

Choo - choo choo - choo - choo - choo - choo.

Choo - choo choo - choo - choo - choo - choo.

C Section: (train whistle)

Woo - woo Woo - woo

Woo - woo - woo.

D Section: (triangle)

ding - ding! ding - ding!

ding - ding

Teacher Note:
Sections B, C, and D
accompany Section A.
Have small groups of
students play these
sections, and accompany
the class as they
sing Section A.

This Old Man

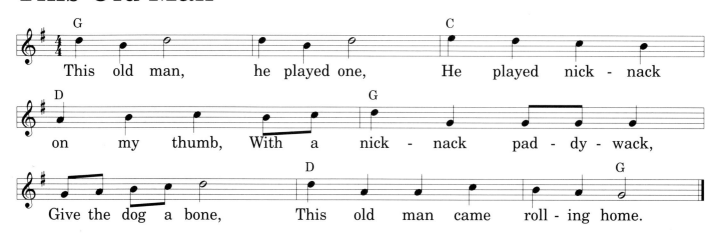

This old man, he played one,
He played nick-nack
on my thumb, With a nick - nack pad - dy - wack,
Give the dog a bone, This old man came roll - ing home.

This old man, he played two,
He played nick-nack on my shoe, *etc.*

This old man, he played three,
He played nick-nack on my knee, *etc.*

This old man, he played four,
He played nick-nack on my door, *etc.*

This old man, he played five,
He played nick-nack on my hive, *etc.*

This old man, he played six,
He played nick-nack on my sticks, *etc.*

This old man, he played seven,
He played nick-nack in my heaven, *etc.*

This old man, he played eight,
He played nick-nack on my gate, *etc.*

This old man, he played nine,
He played nick-nack on my spine, *etc.*

This old man, he played ten,
He played nick-nack once again, *etc.*

The Sharing Song

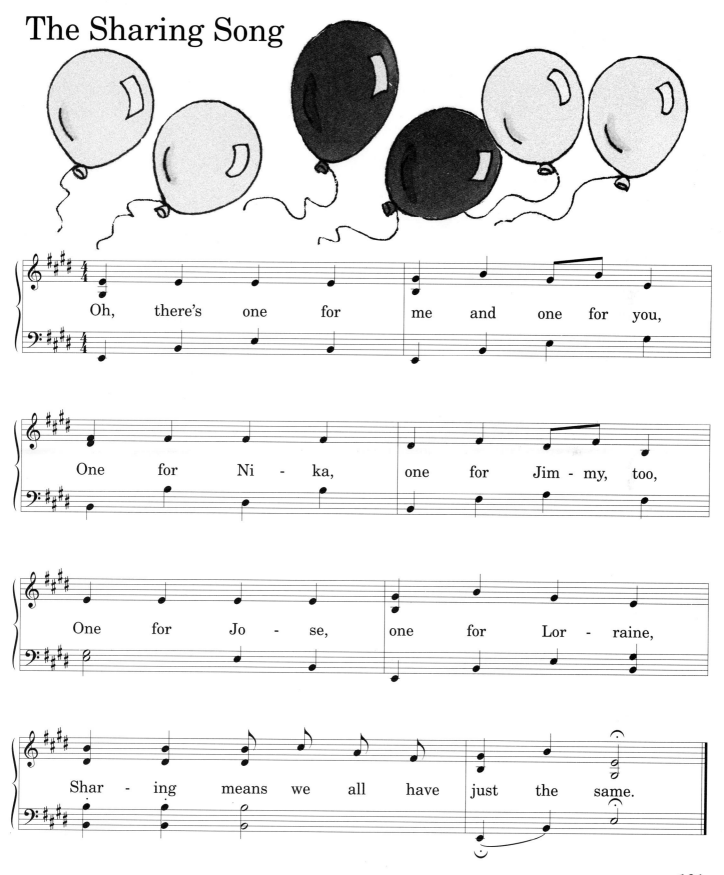

Oh, there's one for me and one for you,

One for Ni - ka, one for Jim - my, too,

One for Jo - se, one for Lor - raine,

Shar - ing means we all have just the same.

Head and Shoulders, Knees and Toes

Head and shoul - ders knees and toes, knees and toes.

Head and shoul - ders knees and toes, knees and toes

eyes and ears and mouth and nose,

head and shoul - ders knees and toes, knees and toes.

Five Little Chickadees

Lightly

American Singing Game

Verse

Five lit-tle chick-a-dees peep-ing at the door, One flew a-way and then there were four;

Chorus

Chick-a-dee, chick-a-dee, hap-py and gay, Chick-a-dee, chick-a-dee, fly a-way.

2. Four little chickadees sitting on a tree,
   One flew away and then there were three;
   Chickadee, chickadee, happy and gay,
   Chickadee, chickadee, fly away.

3. Three little chickadees looking at you,
   One flew away and then there were two;
   Chickadee, chickadee, happy and gay,
   Chickadee, chickadee, fly away.

4. Two little chickadees sitting in the sun,
   One flew away and then there was one;
   Chickadee, chickadee, happy and gay,
   Chickadee, chickadee, fly away.

5. One little chickadee left all alone,
   It flew away and then there were none;
   Chickadee, chickadee, happy and gay,
   Chickadee, chickadee, fly away.

If You Had One Cat

Dee Gibson

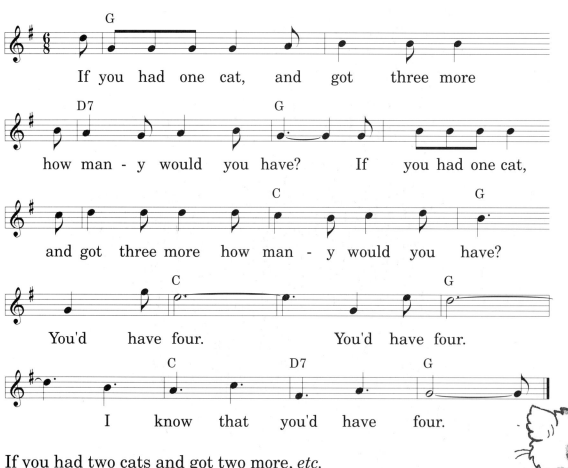

If you had one cat, and got three more how man - y would you have? If you had one cat, and got three more how man - y would you have? You'd have four. You'd have four. I know that you'd have four.

If you had two cats and got two more, *etc.*

If you had three cats and got one more, *etc.*

If you had no cats and got four more, *etc.*

104

One Finger, One Thumb

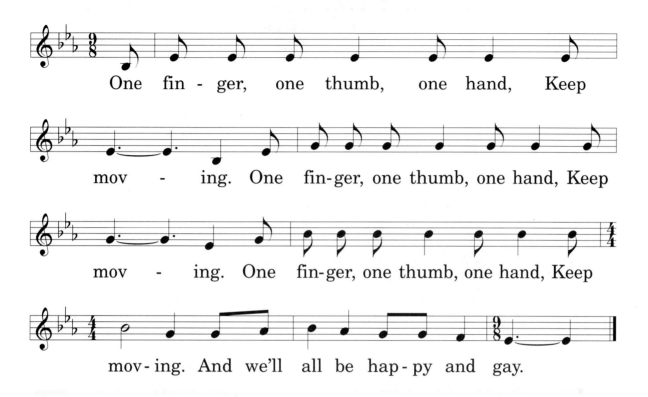

One fin - ger, one thumb, one hand, Keep mov - ing. One fin-ger, one thumb, one hand, Keep mov - ing. One fin-ger, one thumb, one hand, Keep mov - ing. And we'll all be hap - py and gay.

2. One finger, one thumb, one hand, two hands,
   Keep moving.
   One finger, one thumb, one hand, two hands,
   Keep moving.
   One finger, one thumb, one hand, two hands,
   Keep moving.
   And we'll all be happy and gay.

Add in turn:
3. One arm, *etc.*
4. Two arms, *etc.*
5. One leg, *etc.*
6. Two legs, *etc.*
7. Stand up—sit down, *etc.*
8. Turn around, *etc.*

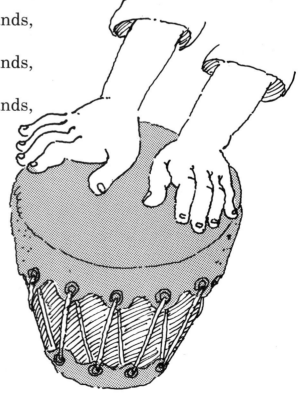

Rig-a-Jig-Jig

English Folk Song

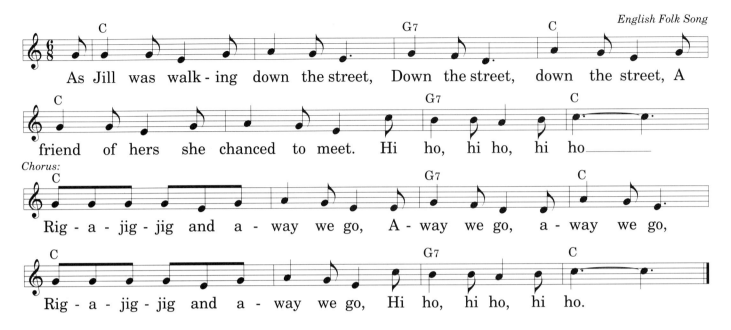

As Jill was walk-ing down the street, Down the street, down the street, A friend of hers she chanced to meet. Hi ho, hi ho, hi ho____

Chorus:

Rig - a - jig - jig and a - way we go, A - way we go, a - way we go,

Rig - a - jig - jig and a - way we go, Hi ho, hi ho, hi ho.

106

The Mulberry Bush

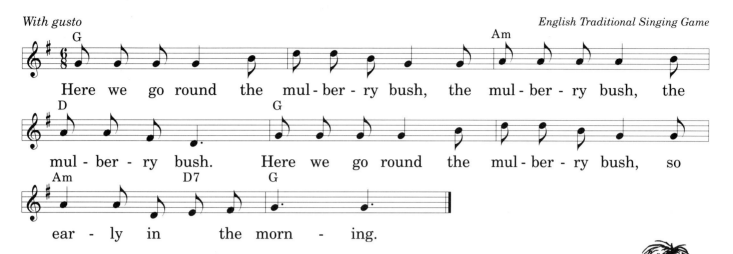

With gusto   *English Traditional Singing Game*

Here we go round the mul-ber-ry bush, the mul-ber-ry bush, the
mul-ber-ry bush. Here we go round the mul-ber-ry bush, so
ear-ly in the morn - ing.

This is the way we wash our clothes, *etc.*,
So early Monday morning.

This is the way we iron our clothes, *etc.*,
So early Tuesday morning.

This is the way we mend our clothes, *etc.*,
So early Wednesday morning.

This is the way we scrub the floor, *etc.*,
So early Thursday morning.

This is the way we sweep the house, *etc.*,
So early Friday morning.

This is the way we bake our bread, *etc.*,
So early Saturday morning.

This is the way we go for a walk, *etc.*,
So early Sunday morning.

I'm Very, Very Tall

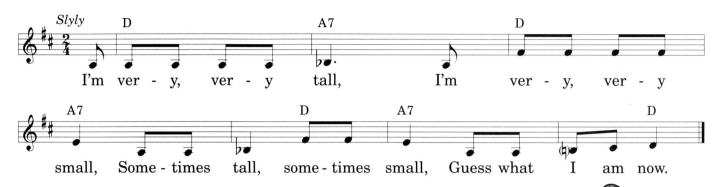

Slyly

I'm ver - y, ver - y tall, I'm ver - y, ver - y small, Some - times tall, some - times small, Guess what I am now.

Bluebird, Bluebird

Lilting

Blue - bird, blue - bird, go through my win - dow. Blue - bird, blue - bird, go through my win - dow. Blue - bird, blue - bird, go through my win - dow.

Oh, John - ny what a day.

2. Choose your partner and
   Pat her on the shoulder.
   Choose your partner and
   Pat her on the shoulder.
   Choose your partner and
   Pat her on the shoulder.
   Oh, Johnny what a day.

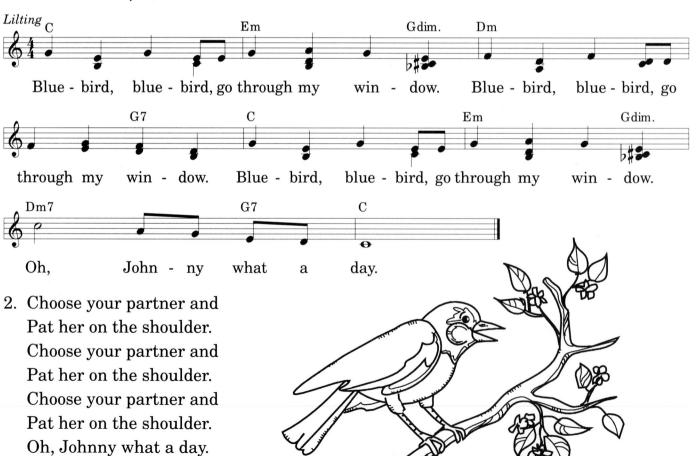

108

Five Little Ducks

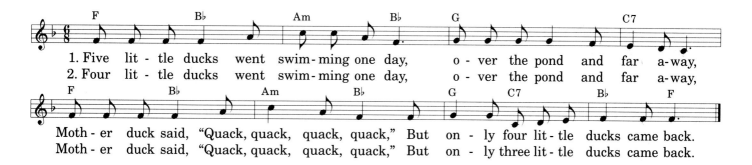

1. Five lit - tle ducks went swim - ming one day, o - ver the pond and far a-way,
2. Four lit - tle ducks went swim - ming one day, o - ver the pond and far a-way,

Moth - er duck said, "Quack, quack, quack, quack," But on - ly four lit - tle ducks came back.
Moth - er duck said, "Quack, quack, quack, quack," But on - ly three lit - tle ducks came back.

3. Three little ducks went swimming one day,
   Over the pond and far away.
   Mother duck said, "Quack, quack, quack, quack,"
   But only two little ducks came back.

4. Two little ducks went swimming one day,
   Over the pond and far away.
   Mother duck said, "Quack, quack, quack, quack,"
   But only one little duck came back.

5. One little duck went swimming one day,
   Over the pond and far away.
   Mother duck said, "Quack, quack, quack, quack,"
   But no little ducks came back.

6. Five little ducks came back one day,
   Over the pond and far away.
   Mother duck said, "Quack, quack, quack, quack,"
   As five little ducks came swimming back.

The Hokey-Pokey

Bouncy

G

1. You put your right hand in, You put your right hand out,
2. You put your left hand in, You put your left hand out,

D7

You put your right hand in And you shake it all a-bout,
You put your left hand in And you shake it all a-bout,

And then you do the ho - key-po - key, And you turn your-self a-round,
And then you do the ho - key-po - key, And you turn your-self a-round,

G

And that's what it's all a - bout! Hey!
And that's what it's all a - bout! Hey!

You put your right foot in, *etc.*

You put your left foot in, *etc.*

You put your right hip in, *etc.*

You put your left hip in, *etc.*

You put your whole self in, *etc.*

110

My Hat, It Has Three Corners

My hat, it has three cor - ners, Three

cor - ners has my hat. And had it

not three cor - ners, it would not be my

hat.

Circle Song

Bryan A. Fitzgerald

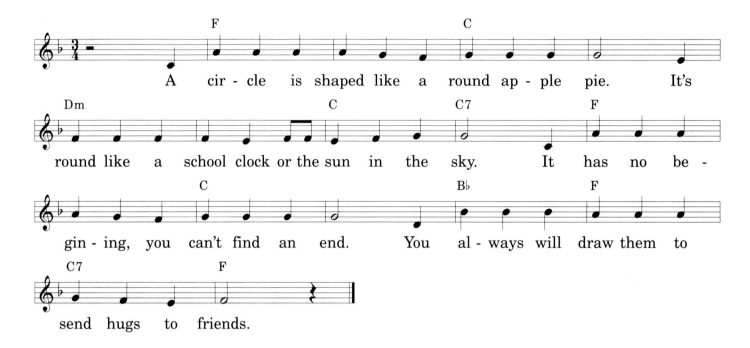

A cir - cle is shaped like a round ap - ple pie. It's
round like a school clock or the sun in the sky. It has no be -
gin - ing, you can't find an end. You al - ways will draw them to
send hugs to friends.

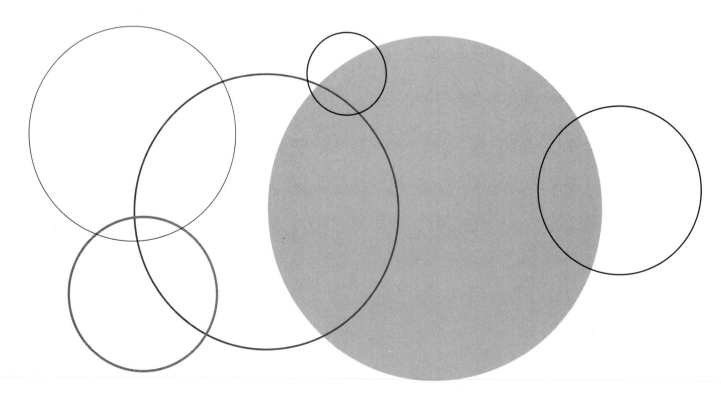

Song of a Square

Bryan A. Fitzgerald

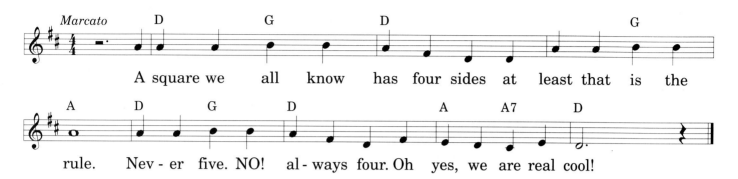

A square we all know has four sides at least that is the rule. Nev-er five. NO! al-ways four. Oh yes, we are real cool!

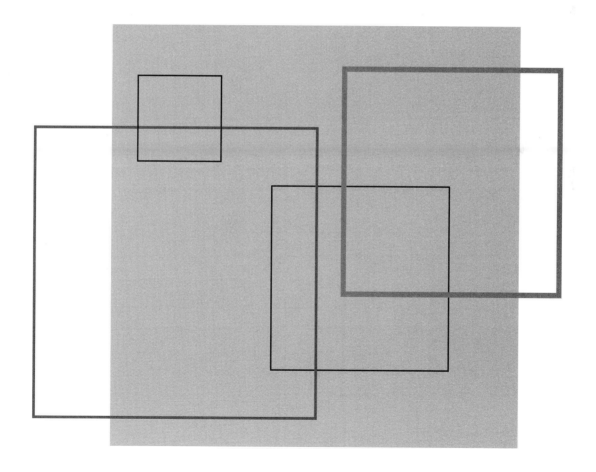

A Rectangular Song

Bryan A. Fitzgerald

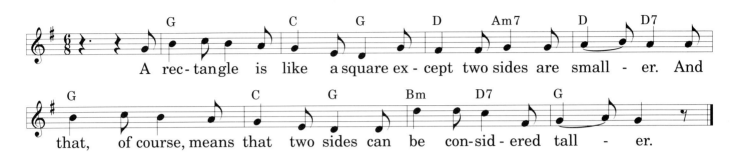

A rec-tan-gle is like a square ex-cept two sides are small - er. And that, of course, means that two sides can be con-sid-ered tall - er.

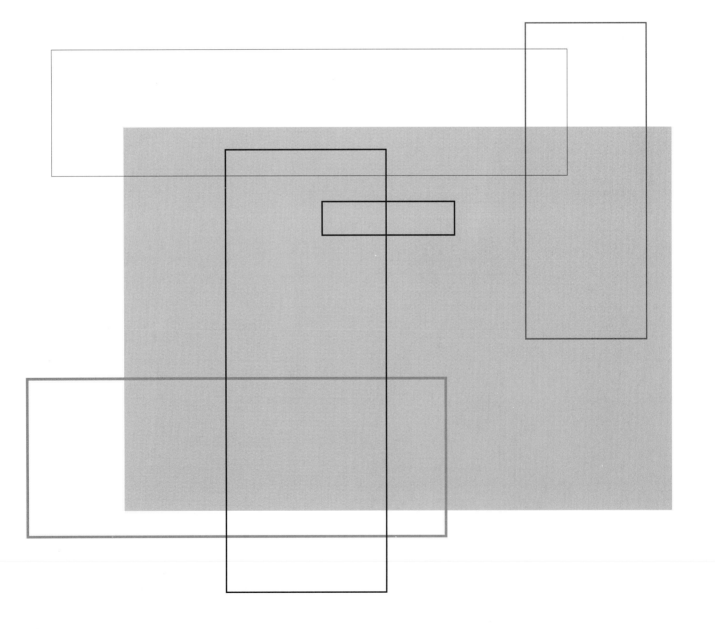

Three Sides, Three Corners

Bryan A. Fitzgerald

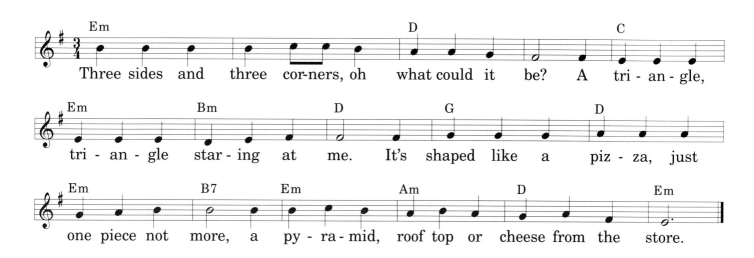

Three sides and three cor-ners, oh what could it be? A tri - an - gle,

tri - an - gle star - ing at me. It's shaped like a piz - za, just

one piece not more, a py - ra - mid, roof top or cheese from the store.

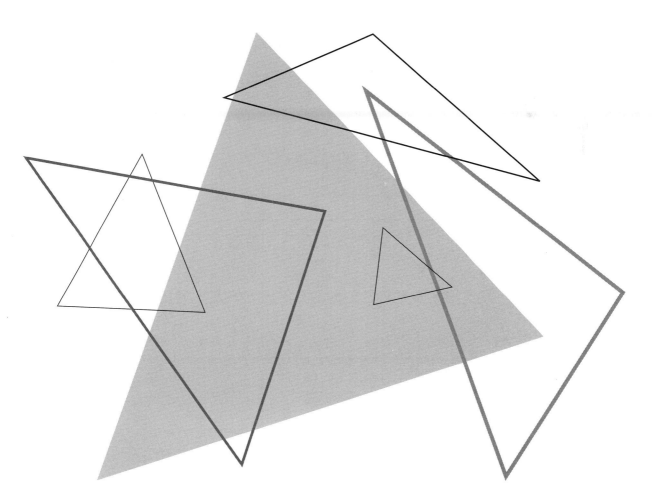

Gum-Ball Machine

Lois Lunt Metz

Lively

My Mom gave me some pen - nies, And told me they were mine. I

put them in my pock- et, And I knew that there were nine. I walk'd down to the store, The ma-

chine stood by the wall. I put a pen - ny in the slot. Down roll'd a gum - ball.

Pen - nies, pen - nies, one and all. I put the pen - ny in the slot to get a gum - ball.

Wheels

Sylvia Worth Van Clief and Florence Parry Heide

Brightly

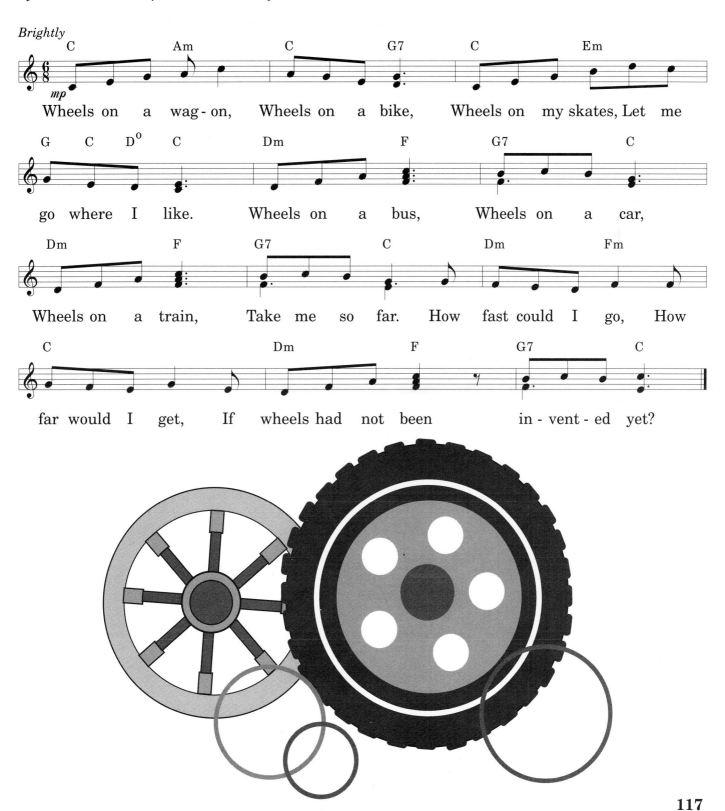

Wheels on a wag-on, Wheels on a bike, Wheels on my skates, Let me go where I like. Wheels on a bus, Wheels on a car, Wheels on a train, Take me so far. How fast could I go, How far would I get, If wheels had not been in-vent-ed yet?

Did You Ever See a Lassie?

English Traditional Singing Game

Gaily

F   C7

Did you ev - er see a lass - ie, a lass - ie, a

F   C7

lass - ie, Did you ev - er see a lass - ie go this way and

F   C   F   C   F

that? Go this way and that way, And this way and that way, Did you

F   C7   F

ev - er see a lass - ie Go this way and that?

Springtime

A Korean Folk Song

E he ya! Springtime, springtime,
beautiful springtime is here with us again.
The sun shines so bright-ly in the blue skies,
makes us feel so gay. *E he ra!*
Let's dance and sing and have a picnic.
In the forest glen, all kinds of flowers are blooming.
Springtime makes us feel so gay.

Read-Aloud Anthology Index

Math Correlation Index

ANYTIME MATH

This chart provides a coorelation of the selections in the
Read-Aloud Anthology to the AnyTime Math program for K-2.

Selection	Page	Kindergarten	Grade 1	Grade 2
POEMS AND RHYMES				
Two Friends	2			Logic
I Like Dogs	2		Logic	
Five Little Chickens	3	Logic		
I Like Cars	4		Working with Data	
Dogs	4	Working with Data		
Tails	5		Number Sense	
The Furry Ones	6	Working with Data		Working with Data
Favorite Flower	7		Working with Data	
Choosing Shoes	8	Working with Data		
Every Morning	9	Number Sense		
One, Two, Three, Four, Five	9	Number Sense		
One Potato, Two Potato	9	Number Sense		
Johnny's Hammers	10	Number Sense	Logic	
One	11	Number Sense		
Two	11	Number Sense		
The End	12	Number Sense		
How Many?	13			Number Sense
High on a Hillside	14			Number Sense
Two Little Blackbirds	14	Operation Sense		
The Graceful Elephant	15	Operation Sense		
Un elefante se balanceaba	15	Operation Sense		
A Tiny Wren in a Tree	16		Operation Sense	
I'll Sing You a Song	16	Number Sense		
Band-Aids	17			Operation Sense
Ten Potatoes	18			Operation Sense
How Do You Make a Pizza Grow?	19		Number Sense	Operation Sense Working with Data
Okay Everybody	20	Measurement		
Sitting in the Sand	21	Measurement	Measurement	
Telling Time	22		Measurement	
Time	23	Measurement	Measurement	
It's Dark Out	23		Measurement	
Tiptoe	24	Measurement		
Hurry	24		Measurement	
Birthdays	25		Measurement	
Feet	26		Measurement	
How Far	26		Measurement	
Bedtime	27	Measurement	Measurement	Measurement
Pig with a Clock	28			Measurement
Our Tree	29	Measurement		

Selection	Page	Kindergarten	Grade 1	Grade 2
SONGS				
The Pattern Train	99	Logic	Number Sense	Number Sence
This Old Man	100	Number Sense		
The Sharing Song	101		Equal Shares	
Head and Shoulders, Knees and Toes	102	Spatial Relationships		
Five Little Chickadees	103	Number Sense Operation Sense	Operation Sense	
If You Had One Cat	104		Operation Sense	
One Finger, One Thumb	105	Operation Sense		
Rig-A-Jig-Jig	106	Operation Sense		
The Mulberry Bush	107		Spatial Relationships	
I'm Very, Very Tall	108	Measurement		
Bluebird, Bluebird	108	Spatial Relationships		
Five Little Ducks	109		Operation Sense	
The Hokey-Pokey	110	Spatial Relationships		
My Hat, It Has Three Corners	111		Spatial Relationships	
Circle Song	112	Spatial Relationships	Spatial Relationships	
Song of a Square	113	Spatial Relationships	Spatial Relationships	
A Rectangular Song	114	Spatial Relationships	Spatial Relationships	
Three Sides, Three Corners	115	Spatial Relationships	Spatial Relationships	
Gum-Ball Machine	116			Number Sense Exchange; Working with Data
Wheels	117			Working with Data
Did You Ever See a Lassie?	118	Spatial Relationships		
Springtime	119	Measurement		